COOKING WITH ANCIENT GRAINS

COOKING WITH
Ancient Grains

75 DELICIOUS RECIPES FOR
QUINOA, AMARANTH, CHIA, AND KAÑIWA

MARIA BAEZ KIJAC

Avon, Massachusetts

Published by Adams Media, a division of F+W Media, Inc.
57 Littlefield Street, Avon, MA 02322. U.S.A.
www.adamsmedia.com

ISBN 10: 1-4405-7956-3
ISBN 13: 978-1-4405-7956-1
eISBN 10: 1-4405-7957-1
eISBN 13: 978-1-4405-7957-8

Printed in the United States of America.

10   9   8   7   6   5   4   3   2   1

Library of Congress Cataloging-in-Publication Data

Kijac, Maria Baez.
  Cooking with ancient grains / Maria Baez Kijac.
      pages cm
  Includes index.
  ISBN 978-1-4405-7956-1 (pb) -- ISBN 1-4405-7956-3 (pb) -- ISBN 978-1-4405-7957-8 (ebook) --
ISBN 1-4405-7957-1 (ebook)
  1. Cooking (Cereals) 2. Grain. 3. Heirloom varieties (Plants) I. Title.
  TX808.K55 2014
  641.6'31--dc23
                          2014012910

Many of the designations used by manufacturers and sellers to distinguish their product are claimed as trademarks. Where those designations appear in this book and F+W Media, Inc. was aware of a trademark claim, the designations have been printed with initial capital letters.

Always follow safety and commonsense cooking protocol while using kitchen utensils, operating ovens and stoves, and handling uncooked food. If children are assisting in the preparation of any recipe, they should always be supervised by an adult.

Froggy's Creamy French Dressing used with permission from Froggy's French Restaurant, Highland, IL.

Photography courtesy of Kelly Jaggers.
Cover design by Elisabeth Lariviere.
Interior art © leslies/123RF.

This book is available at quantity discounts for bulk purchases.
For information, please call 1-800-289-0963.

Dedication

This book is dedicated to the Amerindians, who, more than 500 years ago, started feeding the world with the foods of the Americas. Today they are doing it again, with their sacred grains. And to the courageous scientists who ventured into the remote villages of the Americas in search of more powerful foods to feed and heal the globe.

Contents

CHAPTER 4: Appetizers and Sides 61

CHAPTER 5: Soups and Salads. 89

Acknowledgments

So many people made valuable contributions to this book in so many different ways. To my daughters Patty, Carol, and Stephanie, thanks for encouraging me and always finding time to help me with editing and testing. Thanks to my brothers and sisters—Edgar, Polo, and Ximena—who always worked to find me information related to these grains. My sister, Fina, shared a passion for my work. I Ier passing leaves a big void in all our lives.

To my registered dietitian friend, Maria Alamo, I am grateful for the long hours she spent helping me test and complete nutrition analysis on many recipes. Her knowledge in Integrative/Functional Nutrition and Food as Medicine confirmed my belief that the ancient grains combined with fresh ingredients are powerful healing foods.

Bob and Marjorie Leventry of Inca Organics were pioneers in importing quinoa from ERPE, a community of indigenous people in Ecuador. They have been instrumental in the marketing of quinoa and, while Marjorie is no longer with us, I'm happy she lived long enough to see quinoa become a mainstream ingredient. Thanks also to Sergio Nuñez de Arco of Andean Naturals who provided me with samples and valuable information about the uses of kañiwa in his home country of Bolivia.

My deepest thanks to Cynthia Clampitt, a multi-talented freelance writer whose editorial skills were invaluable to the completion of this book. Many thanks to Connie MacTaggart of the Cook's Library who helped with difficult research; to Lourdes Mordini for her assistance with Internet searches, and Reyna Angeles, who helped me test countless recipes.

This book would not have been possible without my agent Sally Ekus, whose belief in the importance of these grains led her to Adams Media, the perfect match for my book. To the publisher and the editorial staff, my deepest thanks for the enthusiasm and passion they showed every step of the way.

Introduction

Quinoa. Amaranth. Kañiwa. Chia.

The indigenous people of the lands that would become known as Latin America revered these grains, which they viewed as a source of life. Because of recent scientific research, we now know that grains, like all seeds, really do contain the essence of life, along with the promise of growth. That is the promise of these grains.

Throughout *Cooking with Ancient Grains*, you'll come to realize that these small seeds hold a large place in the history of our world and contribute some large flavors when used in modern dishes. In Part 1, you'll learn the history of these ancient grains and gain information on some other ingredients commonly used with these grains. In Part 2, you'll find seventy dishes ranging from breakfast to entrées to desserts that all highlight the delicious taste and textures of these grains.

I invite you to join me—a classically trained cook, teacher, cookbook author, and native of Ecuador—in my kitchen to share with me the joys of preparing the sacred grains of Latin America. In addition to recipes, you will also learn about the tradition of older cultures that, because they considered food to be sacred, prepared it with respect, joy, and love, to the benefit of the spirit and body of the cook and diners alike. I hope you enjoy this journey, which will carry you from the past into the future.

PART 1
Introduction to the Ancient Grains

Before you start cooking, it is useful to know a little more about your ingredients. In this part, you will find information on what the ancient grains are and where they came from, and also why they are important, not just to the health of individuals, but possibly to the health, and even survival, of people around the world. Here, I will also introduce and discuss ideas that are central to understanding the value of these grains and will look at the grains' nutritional benefits, provide some information on food issues and sensitivities, explain how to prepare the grains for use in the recipes that follow, and give you some information on other common ingredients that can enable you to expand on or personalize the information that I include here.

CHAPTER 1

History and Preparation of the Ancient Grains

Like life itself, eating habits tend to run in cycles. Trends arise, adding to or replacing old habits. Some trends are temporary fads. However, there are also visible and widespread trends whose evolution is relatively slow but whose impact remains. Ancient grains fall into the trend of the second type, a trend that offers lasting benefits: the trend of returning to natural, satisfying foods. In this chapter, you'll learn the history of these ancient grains, some of their benefits, information on gluten, and basic preparation methods needed for some of the recipes in Part 2.

THE HISTORY OF THE GRAINS

When Europeans discovered the Americas, they discovered a new world of food as well—maize/corn (the only true cereal grain of the Americas), potatoes, chilies, tomatoes, chocolate, and other foods. However, while the Spanish Conquistadors eagerly adopted many new foods, they weren't interested in what we now call the ancient grains—quinoa, amaranth, kañiwa, and chia—because they were difficult to grow and harvest and, in some cases, had limited uses—even if the locals did value them. Natives of the region that would become Latin America relied on these tiny, nutritious seeds, from which they could make flour and grainlike dishes. However, these seed grains had no gluten, so they couldn't be used to make bread. Europeans wanted bread, and for bread, you need wheat, so that's what the Conquistadors made the locals grow.

But that was not the end of the ancient grains for the indigenous people of Latin America continued to grow and use the tiny seeds the Conquistadors had ignored. Over the last twenty years, more and more research has revealed what these "lost" foods have to offer. Today, an increasing number of people are trying to find better ways to get wholesome, nutrient-dense food to people who need more or better food. The increasing interest in foods that offer health benefits has led to interest in these grains, even in places where people have enough to eat but might be questioning the quality of the foods they eat. Scientists are now exploring the jungles of Belize and the Amazon, and the slopes of the Andean mountains, looking for little-known plants still cultivated by the natives. Thanks to the efforts of these scientists, the world is beginning to benefit from these once-sacred seeds—amaranth, quinoa, kañiwa, and chia—all of which have been shown to possess remarkable nutritional profiles. In fact, scientists, as they work to improve nutrition, are searching the world for environments where these tiny seeds can be grown successfully. Australia has now become the number one producer of chia seeds, and quinoa is now being grown in countries with terrains that are not able to produce other crops.

WHEAT-FREE AND GLUTEN-FREE GRAINS

Quinoa, amaranth, chia, and kañiwa are gluten-free, as is corn. However, this is not the only thing that makes the first four "super grains." Unlike cereal grains, quinoa, amaranth, kañiwa, and chia offer complete proteins with a good balance of essential amino acids, giving them a protein profile comparable to whole milk. In addition, chia in particular offers a wide range of nutritional benefits. Of course, for those who have issues with gluten, gluten will be the most important issue. Contrary to popular opinion, problems with wheat and with gluten are not the same thing. Some people who are highly allergic to wheat can consume gluten in other grains. Those who cannot tolerate gluten cannot tolerate it even when it's not from wheat. If you are highly allergic to any grain, be careful when trying a new grain.

But if your issue is gluten intolerance, these grains offer a way to wonderfully expand your diet.

So what is gluten? It is a protein found in all cereal grains, though it is especially abundant in wheat and its close relatives, barley, and rye. Gluten has a variety of qualities that are important for baked goods and other foods. It helps make dough elastic, provides it with a chewy texture, creates the stretchy network that traps air bubbles and makes bread rise before it is baked, and helps ensure that baked goods maintain their proper shape. Additionally, gluten's absorbent quality lets bread soak up gravy. While there is a small amount of gluten in all cereal grains, it varies in composition, and the gluten in corn and rice is safe for celiacs. In fact, rice and corn are generally identified as gluten-free because they do not affect celiacs. (Interestingly, even the rice known as glutinous rice does not have gluten.) However, these are not the only options available. The other gluten-free, wheat-free grains are:

- Amaranth
- Buckwheat
- Chia
- Kañiwa
- Millet
- Quinoa
- Teff (a type of millet grown in Ethiopia)
- Wild rice

Generally, when a product says "gluten-free," that means it contains no wheat, barley, or rye, or anything made from these. There are some gluten-free oats, but you have to look specifically for gluten-free oats. Oats are related to rye, barley, and wheat, so depending on your issues with these grains, you may have issues with oats. However, if you want oats and gluten is your only issue, check health food stores for gluten-free varieties.

Fortunately, quinoa, amaranth, chia, and kañiwa are completely gluten-free, because they are not actually cereal grains. They are seeds and are unrelated to cereal grains. Other "noncereal" grains, such as wild rice (which isn't actually rice but the seed of a water grass) and millet, are also gluten-free. Buckwheat, despite its name, is not related to wheat. It is technically a fruit of a plant unrelated to wheat. It, too, is gluten-free. Again, if you have severe allergies to any grains, approach all grains with care, including these.

So what makes these sacred grains super grains? Along with the fact that they are gluten-free, they are also nutritional powerhouses that offer a wide range of health benefits.

Health Benefits of the Ancient Grains

In addition to being natural and satisfying, these "super grains" (as well as many of the other ingredients in the recipes in Part 2) are packed with vitamins, minerals, and antioxidants. You'll see the info on the benefits of the individual recipes in Part 2, but feel free to refer back to this section if you're not sure how the nutrients in those recipes help your body stay healthy and strong.

Vitamins and minerals are the elements of food that keep you healthy. Protein, carbohydrates, and starch are not enough to keep humans alive. As history has illustrated, repeatedly and tragically, without vitamins and minerals, people die. (Think of the horrors of scurvy, rickets, pellagra, and other vitamin-deficiency diseases.) Vitamins are responsible for all metabolism and, without vitamins, nothing in your body would work. Specific vitamins do the following:

- Vitamin A is vital for vision.
- The B vitamins (B_1, or thiamin; B_2, or riboflavin; niacin; B_5; B_6; biotin; folic acid; and B_{12}) support your nervous system, help convert food to energy in your body, and are important for healthy skin, hair, nails, eyes, and liver.
- Vitamin C is required by all parts of the body for growth, healing, and repair of tissue, cartilage, bones, and teeth.
- Vitamin D is important for bones and helps prevent osteoporosis, is good for keeping teeth strong, and slows the growth of cancer cells.
- Vitamin E helps make red blood cells and prevents several forms of cancer.
- Vitamin K is essential for kidney function and bone metabolism, and supports proper blood clotting.

Vitamins do more than this, but these are the most important functions.

Minerals are as important as vitamins, contributing to everything from making your nervous system work to building your bones. As for antioxidants, more and more reports indicate that these nutritional elements fight and even repair damage caused by too much sun, stress, smoke, and other things that can cause premature aging and even cancer. Of course, almost daily you hear about the benefits of soluble and insoluble fiber, which offer everything from digestive health to lower cholesterol levels, so you'll be glad to know that these grains have plenty of both. So eating these grains is a trend that fills people up and makes them healthier.

Let's take a look at these super grains individually to learn some additional history as well as gain more insight into their nutritional and healing value.

QUINOA

Quinoa is truly a super grain. This highly nutritious seed contains almost twice as much protein as any cereal grain. It contains all nine essential amino acids and is especially rich in lysine. Essential amino acids, sometimes also called indespensible amino acids, are amino acids, or protein building blocks, that are absolutely essential to human health but that the human body cannot produce as it can other amino acids. The amino acid lysine maintains healthy blood vessels.

Quinoa is as rich in calcium as milk but doesn't have cholesterol, it has much less starch than rice or wheat, and a ½ cup of cooked quinoa has fewer than 100 calories. Quinoa is also rich in iron, zinc, potassium, vitamin E, phosphorus, and B vitamins. There are about 1,800 varieties of quinoa, ranging in size from as small as a grain of salt to slightly larger than a sesame seed, and in color from ivory or yellow to black, red, or brown.

The Incas revered quinoa. Recognizing its nutritional value and energy-producing qualities, they gave it a name that reflected their reliance on it: *Quinoa* means "mother grain" in the language of the Incas. Along with maize, beans, and potatoes, it made up the wholesome diet that sustained the majority of the Inca population. However, this sacred food of the Incas was almost lost when the Spaniards replaced it with the less nutritious wheat. Lack of this strength-giving food weakened the Indian population, and the decline in quinoa consumption paralleled the fall of the Incas.

One of the drawbacks of quinoa, and one of its virtues, is that it grows best at 10,000 to 20,000 feet above sea level. This was an advantage to the Incas, who lived at high altitudes, but it limited access to the grain for anyone living at lower altitudes. For centuries, quinoa could only be found in remote villages at high elevations, and that is where scientists and researchers in recent decades found natives still cultivating and consuming it. Thanks to the efforts of researchers such as Noel D. Vietmeyer, a chemist fostering agricultural advances in the developing world, and David Cusack, a doctor in international studies focusing on Latin American development, quinoa began gaining recognition throughout the world as a nutritional powerhouse.

Grown primarily today on the western slopes of the Andes of Ecuador, Peru, and Bolivia, this high-altitude, frost-resistant super grain is now being imported into the United States—improving nutrition while also helping support poor farmers in the regions where it is grown. It is also being cultivated in Colorado, New Mexico, and Oregon, and in places around the world with suitable climates and growing conditions—generally places where it has historically been difficult to grow any kind of food. Today, quinoa is known around the world, and consumption has increased to the point that farmers struggle to meet the demand. Making it a mainstream ingredient will help increase attention on this superior grain, and people everywhere will eat better because of it.

Quinoa's grains are coated with a substance called *saponin*, a sticky, soaplike substance that is bitter to the taste and mildly toxic. It protects the grains from birds, insects, and other predators. The saponin coating is why it is necessary to wash quinoa before cooking. Today, most quinoa comes prewashed, but because different brands of quinoa treat the seeds differently, especially if you buy in bulk, it is hard to know how much of the saponin coating has been removed (if the quinoa has been rinsed at all) before the quinoa is packaged. As a result, a thorough washing of quinoa before cooking is recommended, unless the package states that it is prewashed (though even then it is not a bad idea to rinse it).

To rinse, put quinoa in a fine mesh strainer that fits on top of a bowl. Pick out and discard any impurities. Place the strainer in a bowl and fill with cold water. With your fingers, rub the quinoa grains until the water becomes sudsy and cloudy. Sudsy water denotes the presence of saponin. Lift the strainer and discard the water from the bowl. Repeat this process until the water comes out clear. If quinoa has been previously rinsed, you may see clear water right away. However, if it has not been rinsed, it takes about three rinsings to remove all the saponin.

Note that quinoa can also be purchased made into flakes, which can be eaten as cereal, used as a thickener, or crumbled and used in place of bread crumbs, or it can be ground into flour that can, in most instances, replace wheat flour. However, when a recipe calls for cooked quinoa, use the recipe for Basic Boiled Quinoa, as follows.

Basic Boiled Quinoa

I prefer to cook quinoa without any salt, so it can be used for making sweet or savory dishes. Because I like to have cooked quinoa on hand all the time, I always make extra and then store it in a covered container in the refrigerator or freeze it. It keeps fresh for 3–4 days refrigerated or up to 3 months frozen. Zip-top bags are ideal for storing quinoa in 1- or 2-cup amounts. Keep in mind that black and red quinoa require 5–10 minutes of additional cooking time. Note that when you add uncooked quinoa to soups that have some acidic ingredients, you'll need to allow those dishes more than 12 minutes to cook.

YIELDS ABOUT 4 CUPS
1¾ cups water
1 cup quinoa, thoroughly rinsed

1. Bring water to a boil in a heavy, 2-quart saucepan. Add quinoa, return to a boil, and cook over medium heat for 12 minutes or until quinoa has absorbed all the water.

2. Remove from the heat, fluff, cover, and let stand for 5 minutes.

3. Should the quinoa taste bitter after cooking (which denotes the presence of saponin), rinse with cold water until the bitterness disappears. Drain thoroughly, return to saucepan, cover, and steam until dry, about 5 minutes.

➤ VARIATIONS

Quinoa can also be toasted to obtain a more intense flavor. Toast for a few minutes in a dry skillet over low heat or, if you prefer, in a little butter or oil, stirring constantly, before proceeding with the recipe.

AMARANTH

Tiny amaranth seeds are about the size of poppy seeds. They are pale golden "pseudograins"—that is, though they are actually seeds, they have always been used as a grain. Each plant produces about 400,000 seeds that have a nutritional profile similar to that of quinoa. Amaranth is richer than quinoa in calcium and iron and has high contents of lysine. It is also a good source of folate, potassium, magnesium, phosphorus, and vitamins A, C, and E.

Amaranth seeds were eaten in Mesoamerica, the geographical and cultural area extending from central Mexico down through Central America, at least 8,000 years ago but were domesticated only around 3000 b.c., along with maize, beans, and squash. Unlike quinoa, which only grew in South America, amaranth was cultivated throughout the Americas, almost as widely as corn. It was one of the sacred grains of the Aztecs, but, like quinoa, it was almost wiped out by the Spaniards. Amaranth was also a staple food of the Incas and other pre-Columbian Indians, but it was not central to their civilization as it was for the Aztecs, who believed it had mystical powers and gave them strength and fitness.

Today, the beautiful and colorful amaranth plant grows in the highlands of Ecuador, Peru, Bolivia, and parts of Chile, where most conventional grain crops cannot grow. It is drought-, heat-, and pest-tolerant, and the stems, leaves, and flowers come in beautiful colors—purple, red, and gold. From the red variety, a nontoxic food coloring called *betalaina* is extracted. The most common type of amaranth in this area is called *kiwicha* in Quechua (the language that has come down from the Incas). Amaranth leaves are highly nutritious and are used in soups or cooked like spinach. Both the seeds and leaves of amaranth are used throughout Latin America, but unfortunately, the leaves are not generally available in the United States.

Amaranth is traditionally cooked like rice or popped like popcorn and made into confections, such as the famous Mexican *alegrias*. It is also ground into gluten-free flour or made into flakes that can be used as cereal or as a thickener, or it can be crushed and used in place of bread crumbs. It is also made into chips for dips and cereals. When a recipe calls for cooked amaranth, use the recipe for Basic Boiled Amaranth, as follows.

Basic Boiled Amaranth

Amaranth works best when integrated into other foods. I especially like to use it with quinoa for porridges or soups, because amaranth is a great thickener. It can also be used in soufflés and savory fillings, and it is great in some desserts and fruit drinks.

YIELDS ABOUT 3 CUPS

1 cup amaranth

3 cups water

1. Check the grain for impurities (such as twigs or leaves) and discard any you find. Amaranth does not require rinsing.

2. Put amaranth and water in a 2-quart saucepan (preferably nonstick), stir, and bring to a boil over medium heat. Reduce the heat to low, cover, and cook, stirring occasionally, until most of the water has been absorbed, about 20 minutes. Mixture will look like a mush.

3. Remove from the heat, cover pan with a paper towel, then cover with saucepan lid. Let it sit for a few minutes until all the water has been absorbed. Fluff and let it cool. Store in covered containers or zip-top bags. I prefer the snack-size zip-top bags to store ½-cup amounts, either in the refrigerator for 2–3 days or in the freezer for a couple of months. Storing amaranth this way is practical and makes using it easier. It is available whenever you need it, to add to soups that need thickening, for making porridge, or in any of the many other applications.

KAÑIWA

Kañiwa, a quinoa relative that is sometimes called baby quinoa, is a newcomer in the American marketplace. Also spelled cañihua, kanihua, and kaniwa, it is the most nutritious of the three Andean grains and is a good choice for those looking for a heavy nutritional hit without a lot of bulk. Like quinoa, it has all the amino acids, including the essential amino acids lacking in cereal grains, but it has even more protein, making it ideal for vegetarians who need a good protein source. It also has greater fiber and antioxidant density than quinoa, and it is rich in calcium, potassium, and iron.

Kañiwa is the staff of life for the indigenous people who live in the altiplano of Peru and Bolivia, around Lake Titicaca. Kañiwa seeds are a little smaller than amaranth, and because they are so hard, they can only be popped or boiled. The leaves are also highly nutritious and are cooked like the greens from quinoa and amaranth. Bolivians use kañiwa to make a health drink called *pitu*—they toast the kañiwa, cook it with water, and then put it in the blender. Unlike amaranth, kañiwa cooks as separate grains, with a brick color that provides a nice contrast to golden quinoa. I like to mix it with quinoa and seafood to make a filling for stuffed eggs or vegetables. When a recipe calls for cooked kañiwa, use the recipe for Basic Boiled Kañiwa, as follows.

Basic Boiled Kañiwa

These seeds are used to make soups, salads, beverages, and desserts, and they can be mixed with quinoa or amaranth dishes to increase nutrition. They are also often used as a garnish because they look like caviar. I always have a small container of cooked kañiwa in the freezer and refrigerator, so I can easily add some to omelets, fruit drinks, soups, and more.

YIELDS ABOUT 3 CUPS

1 cup kañiwa

3 cups water

1. Check the grain for impurities, and discard any you find. Place in a fine mesh sieve and rinse well.

2. Put kañiwa and water in a 2-quart saucepan (preferably nonstick), stir, and bring to a boil over medium heat. Reduce the heat to low, cover, and cook, stirring occasionally, until most of the water has been absorbed, about 20 minutes. The grains of kañiwa will look like caviar and be the color of brick.

3. Remove from the heat; cover pan with a paper towel and the saucepan lid. Fluff, cool, and store in small covered containers or snack-size zip-top bags, in ½-cup amounts, which is the amount I use in most recipes. Store in the refrigerator for up to 3 days or 1–2 months in the freezer.

CHIA SEEDS

According to health advocates Dr. Mehmet Oz and Dr. Andrew Weil, chia seeds are among the healthiest foods in the world. The seeds offer a complete protein; they are, in fact, about 20 percent protein, which is higher than any other grain. They are richer in omega-3 fatty acids than Atlantic salmon—one of the richest sources of this important nutrient. And they have more antioxidants than fresh blueberries, a fruit that is often described as offering abundant antioxidants. They have substantial amounts of calcium, as well as the phosphorus, magnesium, manganese, and boron that help with the absorption of calcium. They contain large amounts of soluble and insoluble fiber, and also have B vitamins, copper, and zinc, and are an excellent source of potassium and iron.

Chia, a desert plant, was traditionally grown in central and southern Mexico and the American Southwest. Chia plants were domesticated probably around the year 2700 B.C. in the Valley of Mexico, a large geographic basin in central Mexico that was the center of Aztec culture. Chia was known for providing stamina and endurance. While it was a sacred grain for all Aztecs, it was particularly important to Aztec warriors and to the Aztec runners who went from town to town carrying messages. All Aztecs involved in rigorous activities, from combat to overland travel, survived on rations of seeds that they carried with them in small pouches. Of course, chia was part of the diet for everyone in Aztec society, where it would be added to a much broader menu, but chia was enough to provide sustenance for those who were away from home. These seeds were so valuable that they were used as currency by the Aztecs. In addition, chia was one of the four staples, along with corn, beans, and amaranth, that were demanded as tribute from the many groups conquered by the Aztecs. Its importance is underscored by the fact that it was held sacred by the groups that relied on it. It was regularly used in religious ceremonies as offerings to their gods.

Chia seeds were also considered medicine, and it is believed Aztecs used the seeds to relieve joint pain (probably thanks to the high levels of omega-3 fatty acids) and to treat infections. The Aztecs would also make poultices of the seeds, to help heal wounds.

Despite their sacred status among the Aztecs, the healing properties of this amazing grain were lost to time until the 1980s when Dr. Wayne Coates, a then research professor (now emeritus) at the University of

Arizona, began working in the field of alternative crops, developing equipment for harvesting foods that were traditionally difficult to harvest. His work took him to Mexico where, in 1999, he and a group of researchers rediscovered chia as a food source. Since he first became interested in these seeds, Coates has done extensive research and coauthored the book *Chia: Rediscovering a Forgotten Crop of the Aztecs* with Ricardo Ayerza. The sudden surge of interest in and availability of chia seeds is largely due to the efforts of Coates and Ayerza.

It's important to know that chia is unusual among these ancient grains in that it is most commonly consumed raw. All my research among the old-timers from the areas of Mexico where chia is grown revealed that chia is always soaked before using. This creates a gel that is easy to digest and is easy to use in recipes (see the following basic chia seeds recipes). The gel has very little flavor, just benefits. The dry seeds can also be sprinkled over cereal, salads, or other foods to add a little crunch and a big nutritional boost. And chia seeds can be stored for 2–4 years without refrigeration, and longer if refrigerated.

Never wash chia seeds, because they do absorb water. You will probably never find impurities, such as sand or leaves, in commercial chia, but it is still a good idea to check for and discard them if found. Chia is most commonly sold as whole seeds, though it can be found ground into flour, and even chia oil is available. If you want ground chia, be aware that commercially ground chia, while a great source of fiber, often loses many of its nutrients in the grinding process, because the large, steel rollers often used by commercial grinders generate a good bit of heat. That said, there are a few processors who are cold milling chia, and cold-milled chia would retain all the nutrients. Chia ground at home also retains its nutrients.

Here are two basic chia seed recipes that you'll find used throughout the recipes in Part 2.

➤ Background Information

The Chia Pet has been around since 1977, but it was not considered a serious source of nutrition until Dr. Coates and his team began researching the seeds.

Chia Gel

When mixed into liquid, the soluble fiber in chia seeds swells and forms a soft gel.

YIELDS 1 CUP
3 tablespoons chia seeds
1 cup cold water

Stir chia seeds into water with a fork, breaking up clumps that form. Let stand for 30 minutes or longer, stirring occasionally (can be soaked overnight). Now it is ready to use in a recipe; otherwise, transfer to a jar with a tight-fitting lid and refrigerate for up to 2 weeks.

Toasted Chia Seeds

While chia seeds can be used just as they are, lightly toasting and grinding the seeds (as the Aztecs did for remedies) is better for those with sensitive stomachs. I know a few people with digestive issues who find chia prepared this way doesn't bother them.

YIELDS 1 CUP
1 cup dry chia seeds

Place seeds in a medium-size skillet and toast them over low heat, shaking pan often to make sure the seeds don't burn. When the seeds are lightly colored, remove from heat and transfer to a dish to cool. If desired, grind seeds in a coffee grinder or blender. Whether whole or ground, store toasted seeds in a jar fitted with a tight lid. These should last for weeks in a cool, dry placc, months if refrigerated.

➤ BACKGROUND INFORMATION

Do not use chia seeds without consulting your doctor if you are taking the blood thinner Coumadin or if you have digestive problems. Chia can cause problems in these cases. Also, talk to your doctor about the optimal level of fiber for your system—because chia seeds actually make it easy to get too much. If you'd prefer, you can simply avoid chia and use the other grains/seeds discussed in this book, as they do not have any medical restrictions. In addition, because the seeds absorb water quickly, if you do eat chia seeds, drink plenty of fluids. Note: If you are interested in knowing more about the medical benefits and reservations about chia, read the book The Magic of Chia *by James F. Scheer.*

CHAPTER 2
Some Key Ingredients Used in This Book

Most people interested in nutrition know that herbs and spices have been found to have health benefits, and you don't need to be told that fruits and vegetables are beneficial. However, there are some ingredients used throughout the recipes in Part 2, and maybe even in other dishes you cook, that may be misunderstood due to conflicting information. Throughout this chapter, you'll learn about fats, sugars, salt, and other common ingredients, as well as explanations about why some ingredients are specified in certain recipes.

As you read, keep in mind that, throughout the book, I have made every effort to use ingredients that are recommended by most health practitioners as being wholesome and healthful. There are occasions when a special dish requires an ingredient that is not really considered a "health food," such as when using it will make a big difference in flavor or texture, but those times are the exceptions. Of course, some things are better for you than others, even if they taste good, and there is also the consideration of amount: You can get too much of a good thing. Following are some ingredients where your choices can make a difference.

FATS

Fats are essential for a healthy body. They not only provide energy but also carry vital nutrients through the body. For example, some vitamins can't be absorbed unless there is some fat in a meal. Fats also have much to do with the preparation of food, making it taste delicious. It is very important to understand the role of fats in your diet, because excessive consumption of fats can cause heart disease and obesity. Heed Aristotle's advice, given 2,000 years ago: "All things in moderation." There are three kinds of fats that you need to know about:

+ Saturated fats
+ Monounsaturated fats
+ Polyunsaturated fats

We'll start with saturated fats.

Saturated Fats

Saturated fats are commonly (but not always) associated with animal products: butter, lard, and dairy products, plus all meats. You must have some saturated fats in your diet to be healthy, but you don't want to get carried away. All the studies done at major universities and medical centers in the last decade have shown that saturated fat has no effect on heart disease or weight gain. In addition, the studies have shown that saturated fat can help control hunger and alters the metabolism in a way that keeps cholesterol in check. Of course, you still have to count calories, but saturated fat is not the enemy.

That said, there are some saturated fats you could use more of, because of their health benefits. For example, coconut oil has been found to increase resistance to bacteria and viruses. Coconut oil helps with blood-sugar contol and can boost thyroid function. In addition, the saturated fat in coconut oil, known as lauric acid, helps with digestion and improves cholesterol levels. It's also a good cooking option because it can withstand high heat. And it tastes good.

Monounsaturated Fats

Monounsaturated fats are found in both plants and animal products, and they'll help you keep your cholesterol down. Among oils used for cooking, olive oil, canola oil, avocado oil, and oils made from nuts and seeds are highest in monounsaturated fats. Olive oil is probably your best choice for most applications. However, while you will want to use extra-virgin olive oil for salad dressings and drizzling over cooked food, there is no point in using your costliest extra-virgin olive oil when cooking, as the flavor is destroyed at higher heat. Instead, use light olive oils for cooking. (Light here refers to color, not to lower calories.)

Canola oil is a healthy choice as well. Just keep in mind much of it comes from plants that have been genetically modified. So far, tests show GMOs are safe, but only time will tell if there are any long-term effects on the body. If you are concerned about GMOs, read the labels and look for organic oil. I use canola oil in some of my recipes because it has the lowest percentage of saturated fat. It is also a good option for cooking at higher heat because it has a high smoke point—which means that it does not burn at higher temperatures.

Polyunsaturated fats

Polyunsaturated fats primarily come from vegetable oils (nuts, seeds, corn, etc.), but also from fish and algae. The most important of these fats are omega-3 and omega-6 fatty acids. The human body cannot produce these fatty acids, which is why they are called essential fatty acids. Essential fatty acids help with cell development and the creation of cell membranes, and they also assist with the building and functioning of the nervous system and the brain. In addition, they regulate blood pressure and liver function, and can reduce arthritis pain, among other benefits. There is actually a minimum daily requirement for these fats, though this is generally only an issue in places where hunger is a common problem. Polyunsaturated fats have been shown in large studies to lower cholesterol, but consuming them brings health risks *if* you do not get a balance of omega-3 and omega-6 fatty acids. The most popular vegetable oils—corn, sunflower, and safflower oils—are high in omega-6 fatty acids; in fact, most people get too much omega-6 but not enough omega-3 fatty acids in their diets. Omega-3 fatty acid is the one you hear about most often, because it is the essential fatty acid most lacking in Western diets. It is the need for this essential fatty acid that is behind recent emphasis on eating more fish, especially sardines, which are an excellent source. However, it is not the only source, as flaxseeds, chia seeds, and, surprisingly, egg yolks are also a good source of omega-3 fatty acids, as well as other important nutrients.

Hydrogenated fats, such as margarine, are the result of a chemical process that turns liquid vegetable oils into solids. They are dangerous because they change natural fats into trans fatty acids, known to cause problems such as an increase in LDL cholesterol (the bad cholesterol), a decrease in HDL cholesterol (the good cholesterol), and an increased risk of heart disease. Twenty years ago, margarine in particular was recommended as being healthier than butter, when everyone began to fear cholesterol (which, by the way, you also need to be healthy), but it is now known that butter is much better for you than margarine. When you buy foods, take a close look at the lists of ingredients, as hydrogenated fats are also found in popular items such as vegetable shortening, processed baked goods, breads, and snack foods.

SALT

Salt is an essential nutrient for the body. Every cell and all the fluids of the body contain salt. All nerve activity requires sodium, and salt is essential to muscle movement. The body needs salt to make hydrochloric acid, which is essential to good digestion. Meat contains a substantial amount of salt, but when humans began eating a more varied diet, it became necessary to supplement our diet with salt.

The belief that salt is harmful to the body stems from the large quantity of salt most people consume today. Most processed foods use large amounts of sodium. For those who are salt-sensitive, blood pressure might be an issue, but an extremely high intake of salt can create other health issues, such as water retention, brittle bones, kidney stones, and strokes. So there is no real reason to give up salt completely, but if you buy processed food, check the sodium content regularly.

When and how you use salt is also a consideration and determines the type of salt used. Kosher salt, in small amounts, is your best choice for seasoning food before cooking, in order to get good flavor. Sea salt is slightly lower in sodium than regular table salt and can help you gain the benefits of trace minerals. Add it to taste after the food is removed from the heat. Sea salt is also the best option to use on salads.

SWEETENERS

Sweeteners fall into a variety of categories. There are natural sweeteners, highly refined sweeteners, and artificial sweeteners. Artificial sweeteners are never a good choice. A highly refined sweetner like white sugar is also not your healthiest option. Brown sugar has slightly more minerals than white sugar, but it is still not a significantly healthier choice, as it is simply white sugar with molasses added. Here are some better options.

Raw Sugar and Cane Juice

Sugar, in its raw form, still contains the minerals that occur naturally in sugar cane plants, which makes it a healthier choice than white sugar (though you still need to be careful not to consume too much). Cane juice is simply the liquid that is obtained when sugar cane is pressed. When raw cane juice is crystallized, it produces raw sugar. Like cane juice, raw sugar still contains the molasses and minerals that come from the cane. This is the healthiest sugar to use if you are going to use sugar. It is good to sweeten coffee and tea. I use it sometimes for cooking and baking.

You can also try Sucanat, a brand name for a type of raw sugar, rather than a different type of sugar. It is granulated, so it dissolves more easily. However, the flavor of raw sugar is strong, with a taste of molasses, so you shouldn't use it in delicately flavored recipes. For more delicate recipes, try organic cane sugar which is processed differently, resulting in slightly fewer minerals. It has a much more delicate taste, smaller crystals, is lighter in color, and contains less of the flavor of molasses.

Honey and Maple Syrup

Honey and maple syrup are classic, natural sweeteners that have been enjoyed for thousands of years. Maple syrup is boiled when it is created. However, heating honey to anything warmer than lukewarm destroys the minerals and vitamins that make honey such a healing food. That said, you can still cook with honey, but it will simply be a tasty sweetener, not the beneficial food that raw honey is. Also, keep in mind that you should never give honey to a baby under one year of age. It is toxic for infants.

Agave Nectar

Agave nectar is the newest natural sweetener on the market. It is gaining interest in the marketplace, as it shows promise for those concerned about refined sugars and artificial sweeteners, but it is still being examined to find out if it is as healthful as some of the other options.

Molasses

Molasses is the dark, thick liquid that is stripped from sugar during processing. It is loaded with minerals and as a result is actually quite good for you. However, it is more bittersweet than sweet, and its flavor can be overpowering, so it is not a good choice for subtle recipes or for sweetening your tea. This is why you won't find it commonly used in the recipes in Part 2.

Palm Sugar

Palm sugar has traditionally come from a variety of palms. More recently, with the increased attention being given to coconut milk and coconut oil, people have begun making palm sugar from coconut palms, which is usually sold as coconut sugar or coconut palm sugar. Coconut sugar contains potassium, iron, zinc, magnesium, and many of the B vitamins.

MILK AND MILK SUBSTITUTES

Milk is a good source of protein and calcium, though far from the only source. This is a good thing, as many people are sensitive to dairy products. Today, the market offers a variety of milk substitutes that can take the place of cows' milk. Unfortunately, when cooking, not all the substitutes behave in the same manner as cows' milk. Suggestions are made in recipes where substitutes work best, but you may wish to experiment with other options, depending on preferences and food sensitivities. Here are some common dairy substitutes.

+ **Almond milk** is a good substitute and has an excellent flavor. Buy the original unsweetened variety.
+ **Rice milk** is another alternative, which I don't use often because it is too thin. However, unless you have allergies to rice (which are rare), there are no medical concerns.
+ **Soymilk** is the richest of the alternatives and works well for cooking and baking. It also adds protein to recipes and works best for making sauce. However, many people have soy allergies or sensitivities,

so don't choose this option if you have soy issues. As with all things, avoid overuse.

There are other nondairy milk alternatives, such as coconut milk and hemp milk. I'm satisfied with soymilk and almond milk, but these others are also very good, and you may wish to experiment.

MISCELLANEOUS

For some of the recipes in this book, you'll see that I have used prepared foods, to make preparation more convenient. While fresh, homemade foods are nice, if you have the time, many prepared foods are excellent alternatives. This is good, because most people lead hectic lives, and if you have to start from scratch cooking beans or making salsas, for example, chances are good that you may think twice before making a dish. In addition to salsas, some of the common condiments and prepared foods that you'll find in the recipes in Part 2 include:

- **Bouillons and broths:** Chicken, beef, vegetable, tomato, and fish bouillons or broths are available in many forms, from paste and cubes to cans to freshly made and available in delis. You'll find these flavor bases used throughout the book to enhance the flavor of soups, stews, and other specialties.
- **Rotisserie chicken, sausages:** Make sure they are organic and that the sausages are made without chemicals. I mainly use organic chicken or turkey sausages that are gluten-free.
- **Soy sauce and tamari:** I mainly use tamari, which has a richer flavor than plain soy sauce. It is also healthier, because it has been lightly fermented. Make sure you check to see if the soy sauce or tamari you are buying contains wheat. Many soy sauces do.

When using prepared foods, be sure to read labels to guarantee that the products you choose are wholesome. Also, if you have a gluten or wheat allergy or sensitivity, check the labels to see if foods have been made in kitchens that prepared products containing wheat.

PART 2
The Recipes

Food is necessary, but it is also one of life's great pleasures. Making good food choices and taking the time to enjoy your food contributes to a healthier life. Unfortunately, busy people don't always have time to cook complex dishes, which is why Part 2 offers seventy delicious recipes that are not only good choices for nutrition but are also designed to fit into busy lives. Cooking with ancient grains will give you the confidence that you are making wise food choices, and with dishes ranging from breakfast to dinner and appetizers to desserts, you will learn how you can easily incorporate these nutritional powerhouses into your life.

In addition to recipes, I also make suggestions about the ways you can use these ancient grains in recipes you already have, either as replacements or as additions. I hope you will take this information and use it to experiment and find new ways to make your diet more interesting—and more healthful.

Note: The recipes in this part provide many nutrients, but I highlight the ones that are exceptional. If a serving provides more than 20 percent of the daily requirement of a vitamin or mineral, I say it's "rich," and 10–20 percent is a "good amount."

CHAPTER 3
Breakfast and Brunch

According to most doctors and dietitians, breakfast is the most important meal of the day. Quinoa, amaranth, kañiwa, and chia seeds are ideal for starting your day, as these ancient grains give you the protein, starch, fiber, vitamins, and other nutrients you need for the energy to get you going. They are also so satisfying that you will more easily go the whole morning without needing to snack.

The recipes in this chapter range from warm and comforting to quick and easy, no matter how the ancient grains are added. Adding chia seeds or chia gel, as shown in recipes such as Janina's Papaya Shake with Chia, will provide extra nutrition, and cooked quinoa, amaranth, and kañiwa keep well in the refrigerator and freezer, making it easy to whip up a nutritious meal without starting from scratch every time. And if you find yourself rushing around in the morning, including the ancient grains in fruit drinks and shakes provides additional nutrients for greater energy and stamina. The fruit shakes are made with milk and fruit, but you could substitute yogurt to make an extra-rich shake.

Another comforting way to eat these grains at breakfast is in the form of hot cereals or gruels, such as the Hot Quinoa Cereal, to which you can add dried fruits and seeds to make breakfast even more nutritious. There are also recipes such as the Cornbread with Quinoa Flour and Cheese and the Quinoa Spaghetti Frittata, that utilize processed forms of quinoa and amaranth—specifically, flour and pasta.

Whichever way you choose to enjoy your ancient grains, they'll help you get your day off to a good start.

TROPICAL FRUIT SORBET WITH CHIA

Tropical Fruit Sorbet with Chia

This Tropical Fruit Sorbet with Chia is an easy way to add vitality and nutrition to your daily diet. Great for children, it will provide high amounts of calcium and vitamins C and B$_2$, plus good amounts of potassium and vitamin B$_{12}$. If you have a sensitive stomach, be aware that chia can be difficult to digest, in which case, you can substitute any of the precooked grains, such as quinoa. If you want to experiment with this recipe, you can use any fruit you wish or a combination of berries and pineapple, papaya, mango, or bananas.

YIELDS 4 SERVINGS

1 pint ripe strawberries, stems removed, washed and chopped

1 cup fresh pineapple chunks

1 small banana, peeled and cut up in chunks

2 cups cold water, divided

1 cup Chia Gel (see recipe in Chapter 1)

3 tablespoons raw sugar or organic cane sugar, or to taste
(Note: The amount of sugar used will vary according to sweetness of the fruit and personal preference.)

Juice of 1 lemon

4 ice cubes

1. Place strawberries, pineapple, banana, and 1 cup water in a blender, and process, starting on low and then increasing speed to high, until smooth. Add the rest of the water, Chia Gel, sugar, lemon juice, and ice, and process on high for a few seconds until blended.

2. Serve in fruit juice glasses along with breakfast or in larger glasses for a morning or afternoon snack.

➤ **BACKGROUND INFORMATION**

The French word sorbet *and English* sherbet *both traditionally referred to chilled fruit juice drinks. In the old days, the drinks would be chilled (and slightly diluted) with fresh snow. Both words are related to the Arabic* sharba, *which means "drink."*

JANINA'S PAPAYA SHAKE WITH CHIA

Janina's Papaya Shake with Chia

This shake is the perfect way to start the day! This delicous recipe was originally given to me by my friend Janina, but I've incorporated either Chia Gel or Basic Boiled Quinoa to make it healthier. This drink is rich in vitamin C and has good amounts of calcium, potassium, protein, vitamins B_2 and B_6, and folate. If you have issues with dairy, you can use almond milk, soymilk, coconut milk, or other nondairy milk. You'll also notice that the fruits used in this recipe are low in acid, which is especially important for those with acid reflux.

YIELDS 4 SERVINGS

1 small banana, cut up

2 cups peeled, diced papaya

2 cups low-fat 1% milk or your favorite nondairy milk

Juice of 1 lime or lemon

1 cup Chia Gel or Basic Boiled Quinoa (see recipes in Chapter 1)

2 tablespoons raw sugar or organic cane sugar, or to taste

4 ice cubes

Place all ingredients in a blender and process, starting on low and then increasing speed to high, until smooth. Add sugar to taste and serve right away in large glasses.

ATOLE WITH AMARANTH AND CHOCOLATE

Atole with Amaranth and Chocolate

Atoles are drinks from Mexico and Central America that date back to Colonial times, when they were made by thickening drinks with the flours of different grains, such as amaranth, yellow corn, and blue corn. It is also well known that Montezuma's favorite drink was cacao flavored with chilies—a drink reserved for royalty alone. These two traditions come together in the classic way to prepare Mexican atole: with chocolate. This drink, which is commonly consumed for breakfast in Mexico, is also full of good amounts of protein, iron and zinc, and smaller amounts of calcium and vitamin B_2.

YIELDS 4 SERVINGS

2 cups unsweetened almond milk

2 cups water

1 cup Basic Boiled Amaranth (see recipe in Chapter 1)

2 tablespoons raw sugar or any favorite sweetener, plus more to taste

Pinch salt

1 cinnamon stick (2–3 inches)

2 whole cloves

Pinch chipotle chili powder or paste from canned (optional)

1 (3.5-ounce) bar semisweet chocolate, broken into pieces

½ teaspoon vanilla extract

Cinnamon powder, to taste

1. Put milk, water, Basic Boiled Amaranth, 2 tablespoons sugar, salt, cinnamon stick, cloves, and chipotle chili powder or paste in a 3-quart saucepan. Bring to a boil over low heat and simmer, stirring occasionally so amaranth doesn't stick to the pan. Stir in chocolate. Simmer and stir until chocolate is completely melted. Remove from heat. Discard cinnamon and cloves and let the drink cool for a few minutes.

2. Process in blender on high until creamy. Stir in vanilla and add additional sugar to taste. Sprinkle with cinnamon powder and serve immediately in coffee cups or small glasses.

➤ VARIATIONS

This recipe would traditionally be made with Mexican chocolate, which is created by processing Mexico's cacao beans using methods and ingredients introduced by Europeans, including almonds, cinnamon, and sugar. However, Mexican chocolate is too sweet for my taste, which is why I replaced it with semisweet chocolate.

HOT QUINOA CEREAL

Hot Quinoa Cereal

This Hot Quinoa Cereal is very popular in some of the quinoa-producing countries, such as Ecuador, Peru, and Bolivia. It is usually served for breakfast accompanied by a hard roll. I find that if I have cooked quinoa in my refrigerator, it takes almost no time to make this delicious breakfast. The amount of quinoa you add here will depend on your personal taste; while some prefer an almost soupy cereal, others prefer a thicker version. Experiment to find out what suits your taste.

YIELDS 2 SERVINGS

1 cup Basic Boiled Quinoa (see recipe in Chapter 1)

1½ cups low-fat milk, or almond or rice milk, plus more to finish, if desired

2 tablespoons any dried fruits, such as raisins, dried cherries, or goji berries (optional)

1 cinnamon stick, about 2–3 inches long (optional)

Raw sugar or favorite sweetener (maple syrup, agave nectar, honey) to taste

2 tablespoons Chia Gel (optional; see recipe in Chapter 1)

Ground cinnamon, to taste

Place Basic Boiled Quinoa in a 2-quart saucepan; add 1½ cups milk and optional dried fruits and cinnamon stick. Simmer uncovered for about 7 minutes, stirring when it thickens so it doesn't stick to the bottom of the pan. Discard cinnamon stick and sweeten to taste. Divide among 2 bowls, add 1 tablespoon Chia Gel to each bowl, if using, sprinkle with cinnamon, and serve with extra milk on the side, if desired.

➤ VARIATIONS

To make this cereal creamy, you can add amaranth or quinoa flakes at the end of the cooking time. These flakes are available at health food stores, but be careful! They become rancid in a relatively short amount of time (unlike the whole grain), so keep flakes refrigerated if you don't use them often. You can also make this cereal thicker and more nutritious by adding 1 tablespoon Chia Gel to each bowl before serving. I also find that when I use raisins or other dried fruits, I don't need to add sugar.

Palachinkes with Amaranth Flour

I was introduced to the Serbian pancakes called palachinkes *many years ago, when my children and I were visiting my husband's relatives on an island in the Adriatic Sea. Stana, my mother-in-law, was a gifted cook and loved to prepare palachinkes for us, and they became a family favorite. She served them with a variety of locally prepared fruit preserves, chocolate sauce, and a Serbian cheese spread. This is my version of those memorable pancakes, made more nutritious with amaranth. This dish has good amounts of iron, zinc, and vitamin B_{12}, and I especially like to serve it with a side of lingonberry jam.*

YIELDS 10–12 6-INCH PALACHINKES, 3 PER SERVING

¼ cup amaranth flour

¼ cup rice flour, plus more to thicken batter if needed

½ cup cornstarch

½ teaspoon baking powder

Pinch salt

2 large eggs

¾ cup milk

1 tablespoon raw sugar or coconut sugar

1 tablespoon canola oil

1 tablespoon brandy (optional)

½ teaspoon vanilla extract

1 tablespoon oil or clarified butter, or enough to lightly coat pan

Favorite preserves, jam, butter, or spread, to taste

Confectioners' sugar, to taste (optional)

1. Preheat the oven to 250°F. Place amaranth flour, rice flour, cornstarch, baking powder, salt, eggs, milk, raw sugar, canola oil, brandy (if using), and vanilla in a blender or food processor and process on low, stopping every few seconds to scrape down the sides with a rubber spatula. Blend until smooth. Be careful not to over-process, as batter will foam. If batter is too thin, blend in an extra tablespoon of flour and let rest for 2 hours at room temperature.

2. Heat a 6-inch crepe pan on medium-high until very hot (a drop of water poured on the surface should sizzle). Brush pan with oil or clarified butter, remove pan from the heat, and ladle about 3 tablespoons of batter into the center, quickly rotating the pan so that the batter runs to the edges and coats the bottom thinly and evenly. Return to the heat and cook until the bottom is golden, about 30 seconds. With a spatula, flip the pancake over and

cook for 10 seconds longer. Slip onto a warm plate and continue to cook pancakes until all the batter is finished. (After cooking a few palachinkes, you may need to brush the pan again with butter or oil.)

3. Spread a thin layer of preserves or jam down the center of each palachinke and roll loosely. Put rolled palachinkes on a jellyroll pan and keep warm in the oven until all pancakes are filled and rolled. Sprinkle each palachinke with confectioners' sugar if desired and serve immediately.

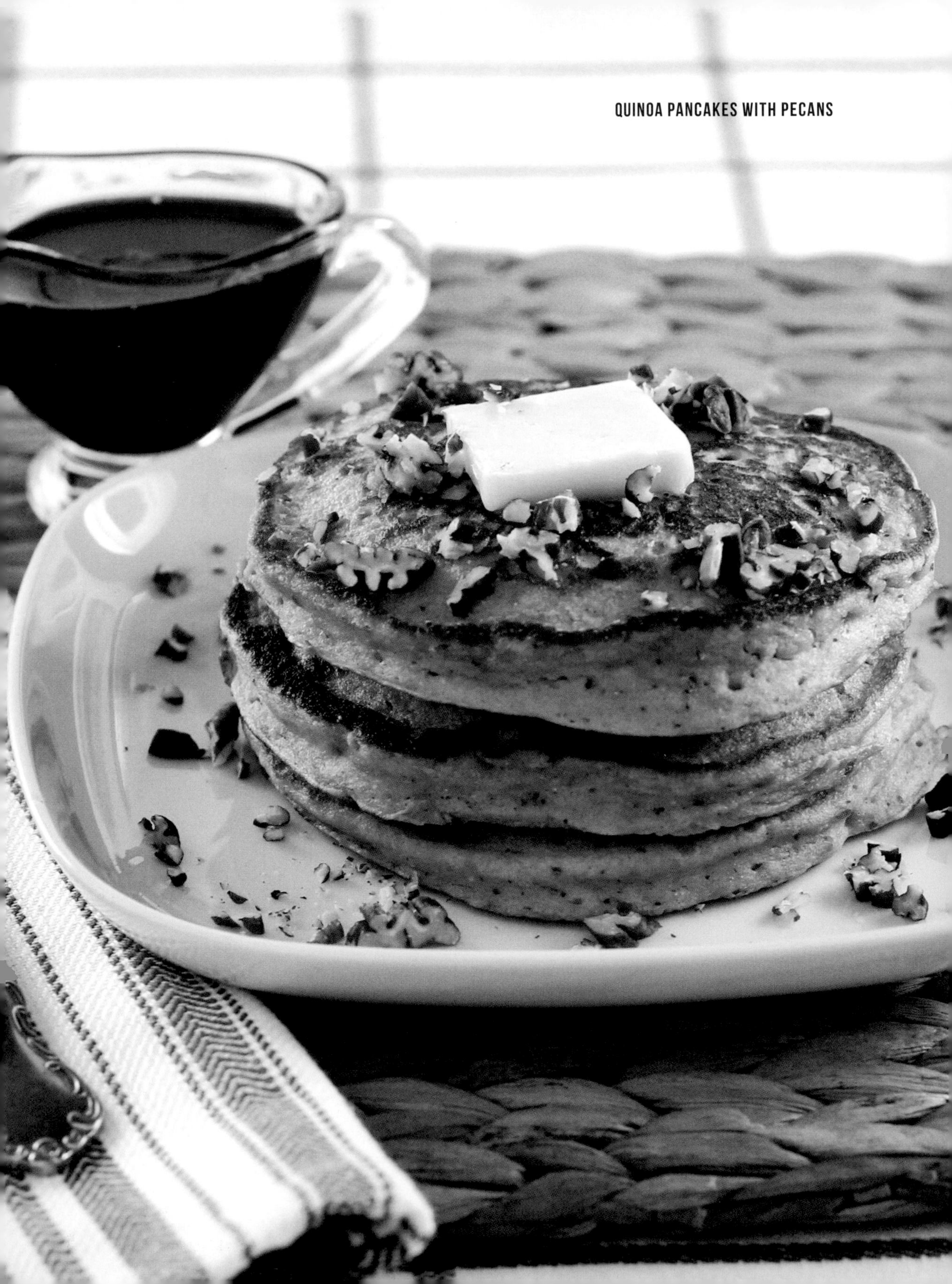

QUINOA PANCAKES WITH PECANS

Quinoa Pancakes with Pecans

These pancakes are great to make for Sunday breakfast. They are excellent topped with fruit, and they're especially delicious when served with blueberry syrup. Honey and natural maple syrup are also nice. One serving of these pancakes will give you lots of iron and good amounts of calcium, potassium, zinc, and vitamin B_2, which are guaranteed to keep your body working well. And they are delicious, too.

YIELDS ABOUT 12 4-INCH PANCAKES, 2 PER SERVING

1 cup quinoa flour	2 large eggs, lightly beaten
2 tablespoons cornstarch	½ teaspoon vanilla extract
½ teaspoon salt	1 teaspoon lemon juice
1½ teaspoons baking powder	2 tablespoons canola oil or melted butter
1 cup buttermilk	⅓ cup chopped pecans or walnuts
2 tablespoons molasses	

1. In a mixing bowl, combine quinoa flour with cornstarch, salt, and baking powder.

2. In another bowl, stir together buttermilk, molasses, eggs, vanilla extract, lemon juice, and oil or butter. Pour over dry mixture and mix well. You should get a mixture that is fairly thick but runny enough that it will spread when you pour onto the hot griddle. Fold in the pecans or walnuts.

3. Heat a griddle over medium heat until a drop of water sizzles. Brush with oil (or use oil spray). Test the thickness of pancake batter by pouring a tablespoon of batter onto the griddle to see how it spreads. Add more milk or buttermilk, 1 tablespoon at a time, if too dry; add more flour 1 tablespoon at a time, if too runny.

4. To make 4-inch pancakes, pour ¼ cup of batter on the hot griddle. When bubbles appear on top of the pancake (usually 1–2 minutes, but it depends on how hot your griddle is), flip it over and cook the other side for 15 seconds until lightly colored. Remove from heat and serve warm with your favorite topping.

➤ VARIATIONS

If you don't have buttermilk on hand, you can make a good substitute at home. Mix 1 cup milk at room temperature with 1 tablespoon cider vinegar. Or if you have kefir, mix ½ cup kefir with ½ cup milk. Then let the mixture sit for about 15 minutes, until it thickens.

Basic Arepas

Arepas are a simple type of cornbread eaten daily by millions of Venezuelans and Colombians. People make them at home, but they also eat them when they are out. Delicious arepas can be found in establishments called areperias, which also sell fruit juices, beer, and coffee. They appear at breakfast, lunch, and dinner, usually spread with butter or cream cheese, and are also a favorite snack for poor and rich alike. Now arepas are beginning to show up in some U.S. cities. Arepas can be plain, but they are most commonly dressed up. In addition to butter and perhaps a slice of tomato, a sprinkling of toasted chia seeds or a layer of chia gel make them more nutritious. They also come stuffed with a variety of fillings, such as cheese, ham, eggs, and chorizo. One great example is the recipe for Cheese and Kañiwa Arepas found in Chapter 4.

YIELDS 10 AREPAS, 2–4 PER SERVING

Basic Arepa Dough

1 cup precooked arepa flour (*harina precocida*), white or yellow

½ teaspoon salt (optional)

1½ cups hot water

Basic Arepas

1 recipe Basic Arepa Dough

Canola oil or cooking spray

10 teaspoons salted butter or cream cheese

Toasted Chia Seeds or Chia Gel (see recipes in Chapter 1), as desired

1. **For Basic Arepa Dough:** In a large mixing bowl, combine flour and optional salt. Add water and stir with a wooden spoon to make a soft dough. Using your hands, knead the dough. If too dry, add a little water, 1 teaspoon at a time, and continue to knead until dough is soft and smooth, about 5 minutes. Let it rest for 5 minutes. Now dough is ready to be used in any recipe that calls for arepa dough.

2. **For Arepas:** Option 1: Roll dough into a 2-inch-diameter log and then cut rounds about ¼-inch thick. I have a wooden press to make *patacones* (to flatten slices of plantain) and find it ideal for making a 3-inch arepa. Just place a round of dough between two pieces of plastic wrap and press the dough to form the arepa. Option 2: Shape dough into the size of a tennis ball and put between 2 pieces of plastic wrap; press with bottom of a can or glass to a ¼-inch thickness.

3. Preheat the oven to 240°F. Heat a griddle or cast-iron skillet over medium heat; grease lightly with oil or cooking spray and cook arepas on both sides, turning a couple of times until a crust is formed. If they are browning too fast, reduce heat to low. It takes about 10–15 minutes. Arepas should sound hollow when tapped lightly.

4. As arepas are done, remove from heat and let them cool for a couple of minutes. Then split the arepas open and place in oven to keep them warm while you finish cooking the rest. If the arepas are too thin to split, just use them whole, like a piece of bread.

5. To serve, spread arepas with 1 teaspoon salted butter or cream cheese, or any other filling you choose. Then sprinkle with Toasted Chia Seeds or spread with Chia Gel, as desired.

➤ BACKGROUND INFORMATION

Arepa flour is a precooked flour, or harina precocida. *However, in Colombia and Venezuela, it is sometimes also called* masa harina, *though it is unlike the uncooked Mexican masa harina cornmeal used to make masa for tortillas, tamales, and other specialties. Look for the word "arepa" on the package to know what to use for this recipe.*

CORNBREAD WITH QUINOA FLOUR AND CHEESE

Cornbread with Quinoa Flour and Cheese

I often have some kind of cornbread for breakfast, instead of toast. This recipe uses either yellow or blue cornbread. It is light, doesn't crumble, and the chilies impart a wonderful taste. If you have sliced jalapeños that come packed in a jar with sliced carrots, chop some of the carrots along with the jalapeños. Usually, the classic cornbread does not use cheese, but it adds even more nutrition to a dish that's already packed full of protein, calcium, iron, and some B vitamins. The cheese also improves the taste and texture. However, you can omit it if you're not in the mood.

YIELDS 8 SERVINGS

3 tablespoons canola oil, divided

1 cup cornmeal, yellow or blue

½ cup quinoa flour

2 teaspoons baking powder

½ teaspoon salt

Pinch sugar

¼–½ cup shredded cheese (Chihuahua, soft fontina, or any other good melting cheese)

2 large eggs, lightly beaten

1¼ cups buttermilk

2 tablespoons finely chopped jalapeño peppers, or to taste (optional)

1. Preheat the oven to 425°F. Add 1 tablespoon oil to an 8-inch cast-iron skillet or an 8-inch square baking pan and place in the middle of the oven while preparing the batter.

2. Put cornmeal, quinoa flour, baking powder, salt, and sugar in a large mixing bowl. Mix well with a wooden spoon. Stir in cheese. In another bowl, mix eggs, buttermilk, remaining 2 tablespoons oil, and jalapeño; add to cornmeal mixture and toss lightly just until lumps disappear. Do not overmix.

3. Carefully remove the hot skillet from the oven and pour the batter into it. Bake in the middle of the oven for 20 minutes or until golden and the sides of the cornbread start shrinking away from the sides of the pan. Remove from the oven and let it cool for 5 minutes before cutting into wedges or squares.

4. Serve warm with butter on the side, if desired. Can be reheated in a microwave or toaster oven, if needed.

Quinoa Spaghetti Frittata

Spaghetti frittatas are excellent for breakfast or brunch. They make great leftovers, as well as lunch for kids, since they can be eaten warm or at room temperature. You can also make them plain in a smaller size with leftover spaghetti. In that case, you don't need to finish cooking in the oven or broiler, because it is much easier to flip a small frittata than a large one to finish cooking on its top side. Packed with protein and vitamin A, and full of good amounts of calcium, potassium, and vitamins C, B_2, and B_{12}, this dish is perfect whenever you feel like indulging in something tasty and good for you.

YIELDS 6 SERVINGS

2 tablespoons unsalted butter

1 tablespoon minced shallots or scallions

1 (4-ounce) can chunky style portobello mushrooms, drained

2 cups chopped watercress or spinach leaves, loosely packed

½ teaspoon, plus 1 tablespoon (optional, for cooking spaghetti), plus extra to taste (for eggs), salt

¼ teaspoon, plus extra to taste (for eggs), fresh ground black pepper

1 (8-ounce) package gluten-free, spaghetti-style pasta with quinoa (I recommend the corn-quinoa blend pasta from Ancient Grains or the rice, quinoa, and amaranth blend from DeBoles)

3 quarts water

2 tablespoons olive oil or unsalted butter

½ cup freshly grated Parmesan cheese

¼ cup chopped fresh parsley

6 large eggs

1 tablespoon canola oil

1. Melt butter in an 8- or 9-inch skillet over medium heat. Add shallots or scallions, mushrooms, and watercress or spinach, and cook, stirring until done, about 5 minutes. Season with ½ teaspoon salt and black pepper, tasting to see if more salt is needed.

2. In a 4-quart saucepan, bring water and 1 tablespoon salt, if desired, to a rolling boil. Slowly add pasta and cook, stirring occasionally, until spaghetti is almost done. Drain, reserving 1 cup of the cooking liquid. Transfer to a mixing bowl and toss with oil or butter, cheese, parsley, and mushroom mixture. Set aside to cool for a few minutes.

3. In another bowl, lightly beat eggs with salt and pepper to taste; add spaghetti mixture, mixing thoroughly.

4. Heat a 10-inch ovenproof, nonstick, heavy skillet over medium-high heat. Add 1 tablespoon oil, swirling so it evenly coats bottom of skillet. Add spaghetti and egg mixture, spreading it evenly. As soon as mixture begins to set, begin pulling set edges toward center, to allow uncooked eggs to run underneath. Continue cooking until edges are set again, then place under broiler to finish cooking, until the top is just set (about 3 minutes). Do not overcook. Remove from heat and let cool for about 5 minutes. Cut into wedges and serve bottom-side up.

➤ Kitchen Wisdom

Frittatas are a wonderful way of cleaning out the refrigerator. Toss in cooked vegetables, morsels of ham, or that last bit of cheese.

CHIA FRESCA

Chia Fresca

Chia seeds are commonly consumed in refreshing drinks, which is an easy and pleasant way to get the benefits of this ancient grain. This drink is used all day, starting with breakfast, and then whenever people need a pick-me-up or more energy. The simplest version is made by mixing water with fresh lemon or lime juice and an optional sweetener, but sometimes pineapple juice or other fruit juices are used.

YIELDS 1 SERVING

8 ounces water

Freshly squeezed juice of 1 lemon or lime

Sugar or honey to taste

1 tablespoon dry chia seeds

Sprig of fresh mint, for garnish

Mix water with juice, sweeten to taste, and stir in chia seeds, stirring often so seeds don't clump; let stand for 30 minutes or more, stirring occasionally. Serve in a tall glass garnished with a small sprig of fresh mint, if available.

CHAPTER 4
Appetizers and Sides

Throughout this chapter, you'll find amazing appetizers and sides packed full of the nutrition and amazing taste of the ancient grains. Both types of dishes bring unique tastes to the entrée dishes found in Chapter 6, but you can also enjoy them in a variety of different ways.

Contemporary lifestyles have brought appetizers to center stage. Whether they are called *bocaditos, tapas, mezze,* or small plates, appetizers are definitely the rage. While these dishes can still be served as starters, more and more people—and even many restaurants—are creating exciting and delicious meals out of a variety of small plates. Many appetizers can be prepared a day or two ahead, so that a busy host or hostess can still enjoy the party. I have been entertaining this way for years!

The side dishes included in this chapter are tasty and versatile. In addition to being good complements to a main course such as roasted or grilled chicken, fish, or meat, they can also be served as small dishes—and with a few changes, they can even stand on their own, as light meals. (And some of the appetizers might make nice side dishes!) For this chapter I have developed recipes that use a variety of nutrition-dense ingredients, in addition to the ancient grains that are the focus of this book. The recipes combine new ingredients with traditional ideas, blending old and new visually and tastewise.

So whether you are planning a party or simply enhancing your own meals, I think you'll enjoy these recipes.

Quinoa Tabbouleh

Tabbouleh, sometimes called parsley salad due to the large amounts of parsley used in some versions, is popular throughout the Middle East where, unlike other appetizers, it is left on the table during the whole meal. Tabbouleh made with quinoa instead of bulgur has become popular in recent years among those who are trying to avoid wheat, as well as those who are impressed with quinoa's nutritional profile. This Quinoa Tabbouleh is high in vitamins A and C, and folate, and has good amounts of potassium, iron, zinc, and vitamins B_1 and B_2.

YIELDS 4 CUPS OR 16 SERVINGS

2 cups Basic Boiled Quinoa (see recipe in Chapter 1)

Pinch allspice

Pinch cinnamon

¼ teaspoon freshly ground black pepper

Salt to taste

4 medium (about 4 ounces each) Roma tomatoes, finely chopped

4 scallions, trimmed and very thinly sliced (including 4 inches of the green)

½ small green pepper, trimmed, seeded, and thinly sliced

½ bunch fresh flat-leaf parsley, washed and dried

¼ cup fresh mint leaves, washed, dried, and minced, or 2 teaspoons dried mint

2 tablespoons lemon juice

2 tablespoons olive oil

8 black olives

2 heads Belgian endive or a few leaves Romaine lettuce or Bibb lettuce

1. Season Basic Boiled Quinoa with the allspice, cinnamon, black pepper, and salt. On top of the quinoa, place the tomatoes, scallions, green pepper, parsley, and mint. Cover and refrigerate for 30 minutes, to allow the quinoa to absorb the juice from the tomatoes.

2. Just before serving, add the lemon juice and olive oil, and mix well, adding more salt and lemon juice if needed. Serve in a shallow bowl garnished with black olives and with lettuce leaves to scoop up the salad.

Quinoa Hummus

Hummus originated in the Middle East at the beginning of the twentieth century. Originally it was served as part of breakfast, but, as the popularity of hummus spread throughout the world, it came to be served primarily as part of the mezze (appetizer) course. Hummus is traditionally garnished with a drizzle of olive oil and minced parsley, but depending on the cook and country the garnishes can also include sliced Kalamata olives, minced onions, peppers, or tomatoes. Pita bread pieces are traditionally used to scoop up the dip, and, happily, gluten-free pita bread is available. However, cut-up vegetables are also great with this dish.

YIELDS 8 ¼-CUP SERVINGS

1 cup Basic Boiled Quinoa (see recipe in Chapter 1)

1 cup canned chickpeas, drained, liquid reserved

¼ cup reserved chickpea liquid

½ cup tahini (sesame seed paste)

⅓ cup freshly squeezed lemon juice

2 tablespoons extra-virgin olive oil, divided

2 cloves garlic

½ teaspoon salt and

¼ teaspoon freshly ground black pepper

Hot pepper sauce (preferably harissa) or cayenne to taste

2 tablespoons minced fresh curly parsley, for garnish

Gluten-free pita bread, for garnish

Veggies, such as broccoli, cauliflower, celery sticks, or snow peas, for garnish (optional)

1. Place Basic Boiled Quinoa in blender and purée until smooth, adding a bit of the reserved chickpea liquid if needed. Add the chickpeas and purée until smooth, again adding reserved liquid if needed to get a smooth texture. A high-power blender is ideal for puréeing chickpeas.

2. Add the tahini, lemon juice, and 1 tablespoon olive oil. Mash together the garlic, salt, and pepper into a paste, add to chickpea mixture, and process until purée is smooth. Add reserved chickpea liquid as needed, to get a soft, smooth purée. Add hot pepper sauce to taste.

3. Spread dip in a shallow serving dish. If preparing ahead of time, cover with plastic wrap and refrigerate until needed. To serve, drizzle the remaining 1 tablespoon olive oil and sprinkle the parsley over the top; serve with a basket of gluten-free pita bread wedges and raw vegetables if desired.

➤ KITCHEN WISDOM

The combination of chickpeas (a legume), quinoa, and sesame seeds produces a perfectly balanced food. This "super dip" is high in fiber and rich in protein, vitamin C, vitamins B_6 and B_1, and folate, plus iron and other minerals.

QUINOA, TOMATILLO, AND LUPINI BEAN SALSA

Quinoa, Tomatillo, and Lupini Bean Salsa

On one of my trips to the supermarket, I saw a chunky tomatillo salsa and decided to combine it with a few other ingredients to make a great salsa. I added chopped lupini beans, which are usually added to salsas in Ecuador and have high levels of protein and calcium. Some people prefer to make their own tomatillo salsa (if that's you, feel free to use it here!), but I often use commercially made tomatillo salsa, because it cuts down the preparation time considerably. Read the labels of all salsas carefully, however, especially if you have any food sensitivities or concerns. Some of them have been prepared in kitchens where utensils are also used to prepare dishes containing wheat, so look for the salsas that are gluten-free.

YIELDS 12 SERVINGS

1 cup Basic Boiled Quinoa (see recipe in Chapter 1)

½ cup water, or more

1 (16-ounce) bottle green chunky tomatillo salsa, medium heat

½ cup peeled and coarsely chopped lupini beans

½ cup finely chopped red onion

2 garlic cloves, minced

1 tablespoon olive oil

1 tablespoon fresh lemon or lime juice

¼ teaspoon sugar

Sea salt, to taste

Freshly grated black pepper, to taste

2 heaping tablespoons minced fresh cilantro or parsley leaves

Purée the Basic Boiled Quinoa with water in a food processor until smooth. Transfer to a glass bowl. Add tomatillo salsa and the rest of the ingredients, except sea salt, pepper, and cilantro. Mix well, then add salt and pepper to taste. If sauce is too thick, just add water, a little bit at a time, until you get the right texture. Stir in cilantro. Serve with your favorite dippers.

➤ VARIATIONS

Corn chips, preferably baked corn scoops or rice chips, make good dippers. There are also a variety of colorful chips made from tropical tubers. You can also try this dip as a sauce on grilled chicken or fish.

RAW TOMATILLO AND AVOCADO DIP WITH CHIA

Raw Tomatillo and Avocado Dip with Chia

Reyna, a lovely, young Mexican woman who works for me in the kitchen, shared this recipe, which she learned from her mother. It is a staple in their home. In this dish, the tomatillos are not cooked, just blended to a coarse purée and then mixed with other raw ingredients, making this an ideal dish for people who wish to add more raw foods to their diets. This dip is a great source of vitamin C, which keeps the avocado from browning, and also potassium.

YIELDS 2½ CUPS OR 10 SERVINGS

6 tomatillos in husks

3 sprigs cilantro, roughly chopped, plus 2 tablespoons finely chopped cilantro leaves and tender stems

2 large avocados

½ cup finely chopped onion

1 garlic clove, passed through a garlic press

½ jalapeño, seeds removed, finely chopped (optional)

½ teaspoon salt

1 tablespoon chia seeds

1 teaspoon canola or olive oil (optional)

1. Remove husks from tomatillos and discard. Rinse tomatillos thoroughly, cut in fourths, and put in the blender with cilantro sprigs. Process until puréed to a coarse texture. Transfer to a nonmetallic bowl.

2. Peel avocados, cut in half lengthwise, and twist halves a little until the pits are released. Remove the pits and save. Chop avocados in small pieces and add to the bowl with the tomatillos. Add the remaining ingredients to the bowl; taste for salt. Add more chopped jalapeño if a hotter salsa is desired. Add an avocado pit to the salsa when it is finished, as the pit will keep the avocado from browning. Serve as a topping for chicken, fish, beef, pork, or lamb, or as a dip with your favorite chips.

➤ BACKGROUND INFORMATION

Tomatillos are actually a fruit, but they are most commonly used as vegetables. Sometimes called green tomatoes, tomatillos are surrounded by a papery husk that needs to be removed before using them. They are a key ingredient in making the green sauces of Mexico and Central America.

Nachos with Chia

I developed this recipe thirty years ago, for a Mexican cooking class I was teaching. At that time, we had to cut full-size tortillas into triangles and deep-fry them to make nacho chips. Now, it's much easier to simply use Tostitos Scoops or round tortilla chips. While preparing, keep in mind that these Nachos with Chia should be assembled no more than 30 minutes ahead of time, because they get soggy. Better yet, serve these for casual get-togethers, and let your guests assemble them. It's fun, and they can customize their nachos.

YIELDS 48 NACHOS, 4 NACHOS PER SERVING

1 tablespoon canola oil

1 (15-ounce) can refried black beans or pinto beans

¼ cup minced onion

¼ cup Chia Gel (see recipe in Chapter 1)

1 (10-ounce) bag tortilla scoops or tortilla rounds

1 cup (8 ounces) shredded plain or jalapeño Chihuahua cheese

2 tablespoons chopped jalapeños (optional)

1. Preheat the oven to 375°F. Heat oil in a medium nonstick frying pan over medium-low heat. Add beans and onion, and cook, stirring frequently, just to heat it through. Add in Chia Gel and stir to combine. Set aside.

2. Arrange scoops or tortilla rounds on a baking sheet lined with aluminum foil. Divide the bean mixture among the scoops or rounds. Top with cheese and, if desired, chopped jalapeño (or even whole slices). (If using jalapeño cheese, you won't need to add extra peppers, unless you like extra heat.) Bake in the lower third of the oven for 8 minutes, or until cheese is melted.

➤ VARIATIONS

Refried beans are available in most stores, but if you don't have them on hand, use a 14-ounce can of pinto beans. Drain the beans, reserving some of the liquid, in case you need it later. Put the beans in a frying pan with a little chopped onion and a splash of oil, heat, and once beans are heated through, mash with a potato masher or fork until they are coarsely mashed. If the beans are too dry, add a little of the reserved liquid. Remove from the heat and finish recipe.

Sardines with Gremolata

Sardines prepared this way make a wonderful hors d'oeuvre or first course. Fresh or canned sardines are widely eaten in Spain, and fresh sardines are one of their favorite tapas. This recipe can also easily be made with smoked salmon, if you prefer it to sardines. Sardines are rich in omega-3 fatty acids and calcium, and other power foods contribute good quantities of B vitamins and minerals.

YIELDS 4 SERVINGS

Gremolata

2 cloves garlic minced

Grated zest of 1 lemon (reserve juice for sardines)

3 tablespoons minced fresh flat-leaf parsley leaves

Sardines

2 (4.3-ounce) cans sardines, packed in tomato sauce or olive oil

Juice of 1 lemon

¼ teaspoon freshly ground black pepper

4 cups shredded baby spinach or arugula

½ cup Basic Boiled Quinoa (see recipe in Chapter 1; black quinoa is recommended)

2 hard-boiled eggs, peeled and cut into wedges, for garnish

1. **For Gremolata:** Mix all ingredients together and set aside.

2. **For Sardines:** Carefully remove sardines from can to a plate; squeeze juice of lemon over the sardines. Sprinkle black pepper on top, cover with plastic wrap, and refrigerate until needed.

3. To serve, spread 1 cup greens on each of 4 salad plates. Mound 2 tablespoons of Basic Boiled Quinoa on the center, arrange sardines on top, scatter gremolata over sardines, and garnish with egg wedges. Serve with crackers or thinly sliced French bread.

DEVILED EGGS WITH KAÑIWA

Deviled Eggs with Kañiwa

Deviled, or stuffed, eggs are so popular that you are almost sure to find a variety of them on appetizer tables, especially at large parties. They are easy to make and easy to carry if you're going to a party. I like to make this filling because it is so easy with the Argentine Salsa Golf (see recipe in this chapter)—and is faster yet if you already have the salsa on hand.

YIELDS 16 SERVINGS

8 hard-boiled eggs, shelled and divided in half, lengthwise

¼ cup cooked kañiwa

4 tablespoons, or more, Argentine Salsa Golf (see Shrimp with Argentine Salsa Golf recipe in this chapter)

2 tablespoons snipped fresh dill

½ cup Toasted Chia Seeds (see recipe in Chapter 1)

16 dill sprigs (from top branches)

32 thin strips red pimento or roasted red pepper

1. With a small spoon, remove egg yolk from egg halves. With a fork, mash the yolks and toss with kañiwa, mixing well. Add Argentine Salsa Golf and snipped dill, and mix until thoroughly combined.

2. Fill the egg halves one by one with the mashed yolk mixture, mounding the mixture in the center. If you have a decorating bag fitted with a straight tip, you might use that to fill the egg white halves.

3. To serve, arrange filled egg halves on a tray lined with a doily or lettuce leaves. Decorate each stuffed egg with Toasted Chia Seeds, a tiny sprig of dill, and strips of pepper crisscrossed on top.

BELGIAN ENDIVE WITH CRABMEAT AND KAÑIWA

Belgian Endive with Crabmeat and Kañiwa

This elegant appetizer is a great way to "hide" kañiwa or chia, to introduce it to people who might be hesitant to try these power grains. The slight bitterness of the Belgian endive is the perfect base for the crab salad. If you don't care for crabmeat, you can substitute shrimp. If you have already made Argentine Salsa Golf (see Shrimp with Argentine Salsa Golf recipe in this chapter), this delicious dish takes only a few minutes to put together.

YIELDS 24 HORS D'OEUVRES, 2 PER SERVING

4 ounces canned crabmeat (or finely chopped shrimp), chilled

½ cup Basic Boiled Kañiwa (see recipe in Chapter 1)

2 tablespoons minced scallions (some green included)

1 tablespoon minced fresh cilantro or parsley leaves

3 tablespoons Argentine Salsa Golf (see Shrimp with Argentine Salsa Golf recipe in this chapter)

5 heads Belgian endive, preferably small

¼ cup Toasted Chia Seeds (optional; see recipe in Chapter 1)

48 thin pimento strips (optional)

1. In a medium glass bowl, mix crabmeat with Basic Cooked Kañiwa, scallions, cilantro, and Argentine Salsa Golf. Taste for seasoning, and add salt and pepper if needed.

2. Cut bottom off individual endive heads, and remove leaves. Select 24 nice, small leaves, and clean leaves with a moist paper towel. Place a heaping teaspoon of crab mixture close to the base of each leaf. If desired, sprinkle with Toasted Chia Seeds and crisscross strips of red pimentos on top. Chill before serving.

➤ VARIATIONS

Leftover endive leaves can be used to decorate a platter for other appetizers, or just put them in a salad. They can also be used to serve other appetizers; for example, fill leaves with Quinoa Hummus (see recipe in this chapter) topped with minced black olives and sprinkled with Toasted Chia Seeds or Basic Boiled Kañiwa (see recipes in Chapter 1). Also, if you want to mix things up, you can use Basic Boiled Quinoa (see recipe in Chapter 1) in place of the Basic Cooked Kañiwa. Black quinoa is recommended, if you make this substitution.

EGGPLANT AND CHIA SPREAD

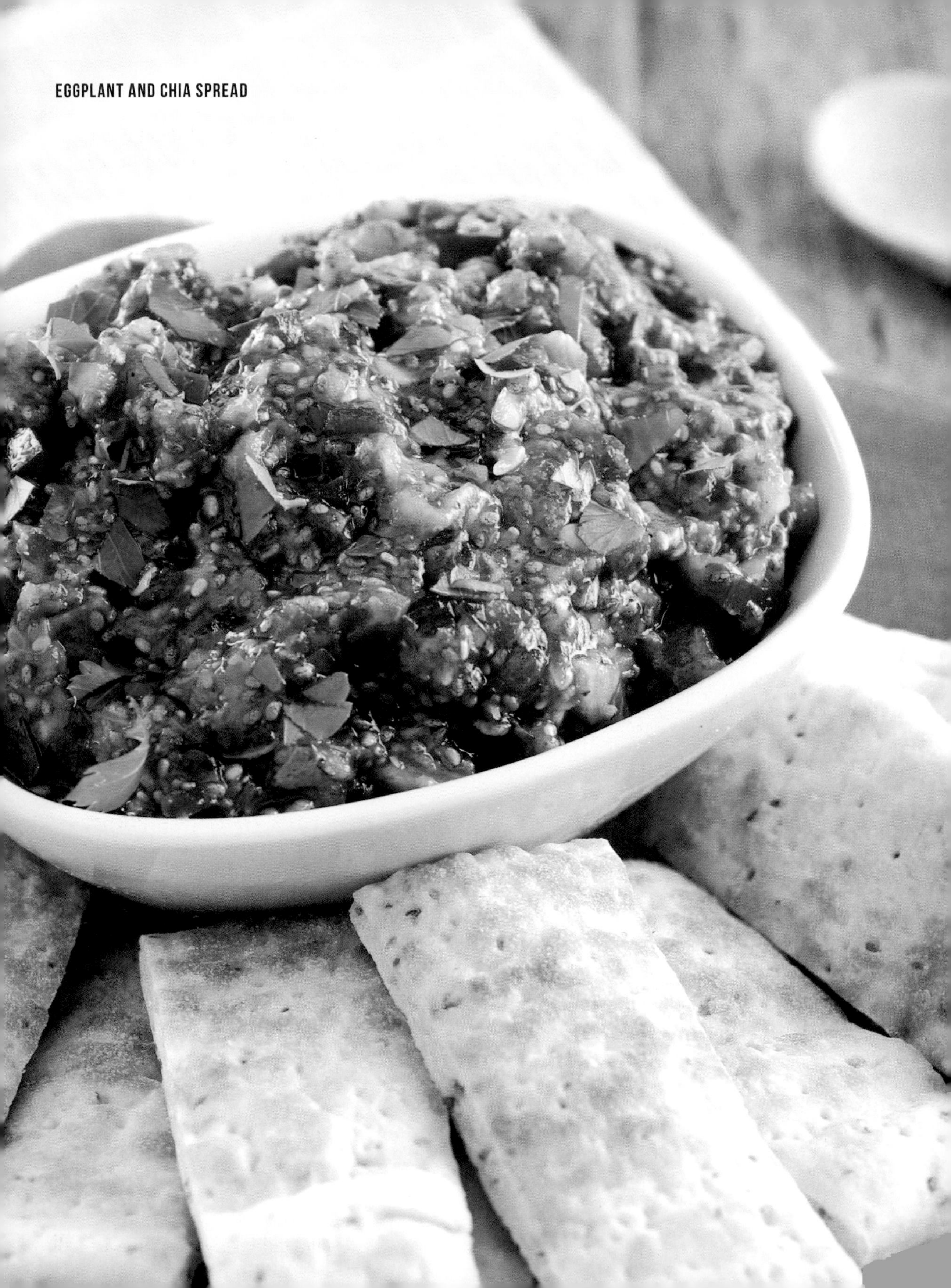

Eggplant and Chia Spread

If you like eggplant, you'll love this appetizer. Chia seeds seem to blend naturally with the eggplant and the tomatoes to provide great taste and nutrition. This dish can be made a day in advance and kept refrigerated in a closed container.

YIELDS ABOUT 2 CUPS, ¼ CUP PER SERVING

1 large, firm eggplant

1 tablespoon salt

1 large shallot, peeled and minced

1 large garlic clove, minced

1 medium ripe, but firm, Roma tomato, seeded and minced

2 tablespoons minced fresh parsley leaves

2 tablespoons extra-virgin olive oil

1 tablespoon white wine vinegar

½ teaspoon sea salt, plus more to taste

½ teaspoon sugar, plus more to taste

¼ teaspoon freshly grated black pepper

⅛ teaspoon cayenne pepper (optional)

1–2 tablespoons chia seeds

1. Preheat the oven to 425°F. Cut the eggplant in half lengthwise and, with a paring knife, make a few incisions every inch on the cut side. Sprinkle with salt and let stand for 30 minutes. Rinse with cold running water, dry with paper towels, and brush the cut side with olive oil. Place cut side down on a baking sheet and bake for 45 minutes or until very soft. Let cool.

2. Once cool, remove the pulp from the eggplant and chop it very finely. (Sometimes, if eggplant has grown very large, it will have a lot of seeds. In this case, remove them first before chopping.) Transfer chopped eggplant to a nonmetallic mixing bowl and add shallot, garlic, tomato, parsley, olive oil, vinegar, salt, sugar, black pepper, cayenne pepper (if desired), and 1 tablespoon chia seeds. If you feel you would like more chia, add the other tablespoon. Mix well and transfer to a nonmetallic strainer to drain for 1 hour. Chill for 2 hours.

3. To serve, season with salt and sugar to taste and serve in a glass bowl with gluten-free pita bread (fresh or toasted), gluten-free crackers, or flatbread.

DATES STUFFED WITH GORGONZOLA, WALNUTS, AND KAÑIWA

Dates Stuffed with Gorgonzola, Walnuts, and Kañiwa

These unusually prepared dates look great on an hors d'oeuvre tray. This nutritious, delicious dish would also work well when served with Spanish tapas or at a Middle Eastern mezze party. A sweet version of these dates—Dates Stuffed with Nuts and Chia Seeds—is found in Chapter 7. These dates can also be made without the prosciutto, in which case I cover the filling with a whole half of a walnut.

YIELDS 24 SERVINGS

4 ounces Gorgonzola cheese or any blue cheese you prefer

¼–½ cup Basic Boiled Kañiwa or 2 tablespoons Chia Gel (see recipes in Chapter 1)

½ cup coarsely chopped walnuts

1 tablespoon finely minced fresh basil or oregano

1 teaspoon hot sauce

24 large Medjool dates

12 strips prosciutto, halved lengthwise

1. In a medium glass bowl, place Gorgonzola cheese together with Basic Boiled Kañiwa or Chia Gel, walnuts, herbs, and hot sauce. Mix well and shape paste into 2 logs, about 1 inch in diameter. Cut each log into 12 pieces.

2. Remove pits from dates, and fill the empty space with a piece of the cheese paste. When you close the ends, be sure the nut paste is visible. Wrap each date in a strip of prosciutto. To serve, place filled dates in decorative paper cups to keep them from sticking together. Serve immediately. If not serving right away, dates can be stored in tins with waxed paper in between layers. Cover tightly and keep in the refrigerator for up to 1 week or in the freezer for up to 2 months.

➤ KITCHEN WISDOM

Medjool dates come from the Middle East but are also now grown in California. Many specialty shops carry these grand dates throughout the year; however, Medjool dates will be at their soft and juicy best around November and sometimes in July.

"Sushi" Dip with Chia

My daughter Stephanie is a talented cook who has a knack for finding recipes that are up to date and great for entertaining. She introduced me to this recipe and I promptly fell in love. This dish is easy to prepare, and the addition of chia makes it even better looking, more tasty, and, of course, more nutritious. To save time, you can mix the cheese base in advance and freeze; then thaw it when needed to finish the dish.

YIELDS 12 SERVINGS

1 (8-ounce) package cream cheese, softened

1 tablespoon wasabi paste

¼ cup Chia Gel (see recipe in Chapter 1)

1 seedless cucumber

2 medium firm but ripe avocados

2 tablespoons Toasted Chia Seeds (see recipe in Chapter 1)

Soy sauce to taste

24 or more fine rice wafers

1. In a medium mixing bowl, put cheese, wasabi paste, and Chia Gel; beat with a wooden spoon until smooth. Spread on the bottom of a Pyrex pie plate. Cover with plastic wrap and set aside until ready to use.

2. Finely dice the cucumber and sprinkle in a thin layer over cheese mix (can be done 30 minutes prior to serving). Chop avocados finely and top the cucumbers with the avocados. Sprinkle with Toasted Chia Seeds and drizzle with soy sauce to taste. Serve immediately with fine rice wafers.

Shrimp with Argentine Salsa Golf

Argentine Salsa Golf is tremendously versatile. It is a wonderful dip for cooked shrimp or fresh vegetables and has become a "must" for many salads throughout South America, especially those that feature seafood and avocado. This version adds chia seeds to the classic recipe to increase the nutrition and add a new dimension to the famous sauce. You may want to keep some on hand to use in Deviled Eggs with Kañiwa and Belgian Endive with Crabmeat and Kañiwa (see recipes in this chapter). I know I do!

YIELDS 8–10 SERVINGS

Argentine Salsa Golf

1 cup mayonnaise

2 tablespoons ketchup

1 teaspoon lemon juice, or more

½ teaspoon Worcestershire sauce

2 tablespoons heavy cream

Pinch granulated garlic

Pinch cayenne

2 tablespoons chia seeds

Boiled Shrimp

2 pounds shrimp, shelled and deveined

6 cups water

1. **For Argentine Salsa Golf:** Mix all ingredients, adding more lemon juice and seasonings as needed. Cover and refrigerate until needed. (Note: If you are making this to keep on hand for other recipes, it will keep in the refrigerator for a couple of weeks. However, if it has been left out, and especially if it has been used with the shrimp, it should not be kept.)

2. **For Boiled Shrimp:** In a 4-quart saucepan, bring 6 cups water to a rolling boil. Add all of the shrimp at once and simmer until the shrimp turns pink and begins to curl, about 30 seconds. The time will depend on the size of shrimp, so watch all the time until it turns pink. Drain in a colander and rinse with ice-cold water to stop the cooking; this will also help to keep shrimp crispy. Place in a large zip-top bag and refrigerate until serving time. If serving immediately, place Boiled Shrimp on a platter and serve with the Argentine Salsa Golf as a dip.

➤ VARIATIONS

To turn Boiled Shrimp into Spiced Shrimp, combine ½ teaspoon salt, ½ teaspoon freshly grated black pepper, ½ teaspoon garlic granules or powder, ½ teaspoon paprika or turmeric, and 1 tablespoon lemon juice to make a paste, then rub on 1 batch of Boiled Shrimp. Put in a zip-top bag and refrigerate until ready to use, or freeze if not using the same day. Shrimp prepared this way is quite versatile and can be used in other recipes, such as the Red Quinoa Risotto with Porcini Mushrooms in Chapter 6.

Cheese and Kañiwa Arepas

I love Basic Arepas (see recipe in Chapter 3) with a little bit of butter or cheese, but one day when I was making cheese arepas, it occurred to me that mixing some kañiwa with the cheese arepa dough would provide more protein and good amounts of calcium and vitamin C. Thus these Cheese and Kañiwa Arepas were born! Arepas are so versatile you can eat them with different kinds of fillings, such as cream cheese with jelly, chorizo, ham, scrambled eggs, refried beans, or any other filling that you have in your refrigerator.

YIELDS ABOUT 12 AREPAS, 2 PER SERVING

1 recipe Basic Arepa Dough (see Basic Arepas recipe in Chapter 3)

½ cup Basic Boiled Kañiwa (see recipe in Chapter 1)

½–1 cup Parmesan cheese or any other shredded cheese you have

3 large Roma tomatoes

Sea salt and freshly ground black pepper

1 log fresh mozzarella, sliced into 12 ¼-inch rounds

12 large basil leaves

Extra-virgin olive oil (for drizzling), or if available, olive oil flavored with truffles (optional)

1. In a medium bowl, mix Basic Arepa Dough with Basic Boiled Kañiwa and cheese. Knead well until all ingredients are incorporated and dough is smooth.

2. To shape arepas, follow instructions given in Basic Arepas recipe in Chapter 3.

3. Slice tomatoes thinly and place on a tray lined with paper towels to drain. Sprinkle with salt and pepper to taste.

4. To serve, split the arepas, separating top from bottom. Then, assemble like a sandwich: bottom of arepa, a slice of cheese, a slice of tomato, then a basil leaf. Drizzle with oil. Add the top of the arepa and serve immediately.

➤ VARIATIONS

If you have any trouble splitting the arepas, simply leave them whole and assemble them as an open-face sandwich. In these cases, I spread a little butter on the arepa, or better yet, pesto, if I have it, or a flavored butter. Then stack the cheese and tomato on top.

Armenian Green Beans and Tomatoes with Quinoa

This simple Armenian side dish blends very well with different types of herbs, and it is a great accompaniment to any kind of meat. The sliced onion is commonly salted and crushed with the heel of the hand to release the strong juices, but in this recipe the sliced onion is boiled with the beans. This releases the onion's juices without having to crush the onion. It also makes the onion milder and flavors the beans.

YIELDS 4–6 SERVINGS

3 tablespoons olive oil

2 tablespoons white wine vinegar

½ teaspoon salt

¼ teaspoon freshly grated black pepper

1 pound green beans

1 medium onion, halved and sliced ⅛-inch thick

4 medium (4–5 ounce) tomatoes, preferably of assorted colors

½ cup Basic Boiled Quinoa (see recipe in Chapter 1; red quinoa is recommended)

¼ cup finely chopped fresh parsley leaves

2 tablespoons fresh-snipped dill

Salt and pepper to taste

¼ cup Toasted Chia Seeds (see recipe in Chapter 1)

1. In a small bowl, beat oil, vinegar, salt, and pepper with a fork until emulsified. Set aside. If you desire less acidity, add more oil.

2. Wash green beans and snap off the ends, pulling down the strings. Cut into 1-inch pieces, drop into salted boiling water along with onion slices, and cook, uncovered, for 4–5 minutes, or until crisp-tender. Drain and rinse under cold running water. Dry, put in a plastic bag, and refrigerate.

3. Rinse tomatoes and core. Cut in half across, gently squeeze to remove excess liquid, cut into bite-size pieces, and transfer to a bowl. Cover and refrigerate until needed.

4. To assemble dish, place green beans, tomatoes, and Basic Boiled Quinoa in a mixing bowl, add parsley and dill, and toss with oil and vinegar dressing. Add salt and pepper to taste. Sprinkle with Toasted Chia Seeds.

➤ KITCHEN WISDOM

Tomatoes begin to deteriorate rapidly if they are kept in the refrigerator. It's okay to chill them for a few minutes while you're preparing other items, but don't let them languish for hours.

MOROCCAN-STYLE QUINOA WITH DRIED FRUITS AND NUTS

Moroccan-Style Quinoa with Dried Fruits and Nuts

The source of my inspiration for this recipe was The African and Middle Eastern Cookbook *by Josephine Bacon and Jenni Fleetwood. This specialty is normally made with couscous, which is a staple throughout Algeria, Morocco, and Tunisia. I make this version of the dish with quinoa instead of couscous, and it is the perfect accompaniment to any kind of poultry or pork dish. In Morocco this dish is usually served as part of a celebration meal, as a course of its own. I often use it to stuff Cornish hens, and then bake the remaining quinoa mixture in a separate bowl.*

YIELDS 6 SERVINGS

1 cup raw quinoa, thoroughly rinsed

1¾ cups water

½ teaspoon salt

½ teaspoon crumbled saffron threads

1 tablespoon canola oil

1 tablespoon unsalted butter

6 dried apricots cut into slivers

¼ cup diced dried figs (any kind) or dried cranberries

¼ cup golden seedless raisins

½ cup sliced blanched almonds

¼ cup pistachio nuts

1 tablespoon superfine sugar, for garnish

1 teaspoon ground cinnamon, for garnish

1. Preheat the oven to 350°F.

2. Place quinoa in a 2-quart saucepan, add water, and mix in salt and saffron threads. Bring to a boil over medium heat, cover, and simmer for 12 minutes or until quinoa has absorbed all the liquid. Remove from the heat, fluff with a fork, cover, and let rest for 5 minutes.

3. In a large skillet, heat canola oil and butter over medium heat. Add the apricots, figs, raisins, almonds, and pistachios; cook, stirring occasionally, until the raisins plump up, about 3–5 minutes, depending on how dry raisins are. Add to quinoa, mix well, and transfer to an ovenproof shallow baking dish. Note: If making ahead of time, cool, cover, and refrigerate until needed, then remove from refrigerator and bring to room temperature before moving on to the next step.

4. Bake in the middle of a preheated oven for 20 minutes or until heated through. Remove from heat, transfer to a serving dish, and pile quinoa into a cone-shaped mound. Mix sugar and cinnamon together and sprinkle in stripes down the mound.

➤ **BACKGROUND INFORMATION**

Combining sweet and savory flavors in one dish is common in Arab cuisine. Famous, savory Moroccan dishes, such as bastilla, a pigeon or chicken pie, are sprinkled with cinnamon and sugar. Adding fruit and nuts to meats or grains are also classic elements in Moroccan cooking.

PICO DE GALLO WITH MANGO AND CHIA

Pico de Gallo with Mango and Chia

Traditional pico de gallo, made with tomatoes, chilies, and onions, is a familiar condiment among those who enjoy Mexican food. This new version features two additional ingredients not found in the classic pico de gallo—mango and cucumber. These additions give this salsa a refreshing and delicious taste, toning down the heat of the chilies. They also add extra color and nutrition, making this dish rich in vitamins C and A. Use this Pico de Gallo with Mango and Chia to dress up poultry, pork, and meaty grilled fish such as tuna.

YIELDS ABOUT 3 CUPS OR 12 SERVINGS

2 firm Manila mangoes, peeled, pit removed, cut into ¼-inch dice (about 1 cup)

1 large plum tomato, seeded and chopped into ¼-inch dice (about ¾ cup)

1 small pickling cucumber, diced ¼ inch (about ¾ cup)

1 small white onion, preferably Vidalia, finely chopped (about 1 cup)

½ cup (or more) Chia Gel or Basic Boiled Quinoa (black quinoa is recommended; see recipes in Chapter 1)

1 or 2 serrano chilies, seeded and minced (or use 1 medium jalapeño)

3 tablespoons fresh lime juice

1 tablespoon olive oil

¼ teaspoon salt

¼ teaspoon freshly ground black pepper

2 tablespoons fresh minced cilantro leaves, or parsley and mint combined.

1. In a medium bowl, mix all the ingredients, adding more salt and lime juice if needed. Store in a glass container, cover, and refrigerate until needed.

2. Serve in a glass or ceramic bowl with black corn chips, corn scoops, or any gluten-free dipper.

➤ KITCHEN WISDOM

Manila mangoes, also called Champagne mangoes, are becoming more and more available at supermarkets. They are yellow in color, and smaller than the Florida mangoes, with great texture and taste. Use these if available.

QUINOA PILAF WITH PEAS, PINE NUTS, AND CURRANTS

Quinoa Pilaf with Peas, Pine Nuts, and Currants

There are dishes that quickly become a favorite with cooks, because of their taste and versatility. For me, this is one of those dishes. Even people who are reluctant to try new foods love this Quinoa Pilaf with Peas, Pine Nuts, and Currants, which is packed full of iron and vitamin C. It is extremely versatile, and is a terrific complement to chicken, fish, or meat, as well as to spicy dishes. It can also be used as a stuffing for quail or chicken.

YIELDS ABOUT 5 CUPS, ½ CUP PER SERVING

1 cup raw quinoa, thoroughly rinsed

1¾ cups low-salt vegetable broth or bouillon made with 1 bouillon cube

1 bruised garlic clove

1 teaspoon ground turmeric

1 tablespoon olive oil

2 tablespoons unsalted butter

⅓ cup pine nuts

¼ cup currants

½ cup finely chopped scallions (white part with 1 inch of the green)

½ cup minced fresh parsley leaves

1 cup cooked fresh peas or frozen petits pois

¼ teaspoon freshly ground black pepper

1. Put quinoa in a 2-quart saucepan. Stir in broth/bouillon, garlic clove, turmeric, and olive oil, and bring to a boil over medium heat. Cook over medium heat for 12 minutes or until quinoa has absorbed all the water. Remove from the heat, fluff, cover, and let stand for 5 minutes.

2. Heat butter in a large skillet. Add pine nuts and cook for 30 seconds. Add currants, scallions, parsley, and peas, and cook for 30 more seconds, stirring once. Add quinoa and ground pepper, and cook, stirring, until heated through, about 3–5 minutes. Serve hot.

CHAPTER 5
Soups and Salads

Few other dishes are as accommodating of these grains as soup. Quinoa can be used in any soups including vegetable soups, soups with or without meat, in creamed soups, or as a garnish instead of croutons. You can also substitute quinoa or quinoa pasta in any recipe where you now use pasta, bulgur, or rice. Amaranth and kañiwa, on the other hand, are ideal for creamed soups because of their small size, especially amaranth, which turns into mush after cooking and becomes a great thickener. And let's not forget quinoa or amaranth flakes, which come in very handy if the consistency of the soup is too thin. You can simply add tablespoons of either to taste at the end of the cooking time, to thicken the soup and make it creamier. In addition, if there is too much liquid in a soup, you can add 3 or 4 tablespoons of chia seeds, and wait 15–20 minutes for the extra liquid to be absorbed. This will not give you the creaminess that flakes offer, but it will keep the soup from being watery. Any of these grains can be combined for varied textures and even greater nutritional benefits. And, as a bonus, all these soups freeze very well, so you can fill your freezer and be ready to enjoy a wholesome soup at any time.

Of course, the combination of soup and salad is classic, so this section includes a wonderful range of salads, as well. While the salads included are varied—ranging from Quinoa Salad with Corn and Black Beans to Roasted Beets with Fresh Mozzarella Balls to Seven-Vegetable Salad with Quinoa and Kañiwa—many offer the opportunity to incorporate raw vegetables into your diet. However, all vegetables, raw or cooked, in a rainbow of colors, are wonderful for improving your health—plus, in these salads, they are just delicious.

Wild Rice with Quinoa or Kañiwa Soup

This fine soup is especially popular in Minnesota, where wild rice is the official state grain. It's packed full of vitamin A and has good amounts of B_{12} and niacin. If you like a more intense mushroom taste, wild mushrooms (fresh or rehydrated dried) can be added to the soup along with the baby portobello mushrooms. Some cooks flavor the soup with diced bacon, Canadian bacon, or sliced smoked chicken. If using any of these meats, add at the same time you add the mushrooms. As with most soups, this improves overnight.

YIELDS 10 1-CUP SERVINGS

4 cups water, divided

½ cup wild rice, thoroughly rinsed

½ cup raw quinoa or kañiwa, well rinsed

2 tablespoons canola oil

1 medium onion, minced (about 1 cup)

1 large celery stick, thinly sliced (about 1 cup)

¾ cup finely chopped red bell pepper

1 large carrot, finely chopped (about ¾ cup)

3 cloves garlic, passed through a garlic press

1 (4–6 ounce) can baby portobello mushrooms, coarsely chopped

1 teaspoon salt

½ teaspoon freshly ground black pepper

¼ teaspoon dry thyme

¼ teaspoon dry red pepper flakes

2 tablespoons quinoa flour

2 cups hot water

1 (32-ounce) carton (4 cups) low-sodium beef broth

1 pint half-and-half

3 tablespoons dry sherry (optional)

Juice of 1 lime

1. Bring 3 cups water to a boil in a 2-quart saucepan. Add wild rice and simmer, covered, until grains are almost tender, about 25 minutes. Drain, cover, and set aside.

2. In a small saucepan, cook quinoa or kañiwa in 1 cup water for 15 minutes, or until most of the water has been absorbed.

3. In a 4-quart saucepan or casserole, heat oil over medium heat. Add onions, celery, red bell pepper, carrots, garlic, and mushrooms; cook, stirring occasionally, for 5 minutes. Season with salt, black pepper, thyme, and red pepper flakes. Stir in quinoa flour and cook for 1 minute. Beat in hot water, stirring constantly until sauce is smooth. Add beef broth, wild rice, and quinoa or kañiwa, and bring to a boil. Reduce the heat and simmer for 15 minutes or until vegetables are done. Add half-and-half, sherry (if using), and lime juice, and slowly return to a boil. Add salt to taste. Remove from the heat.

4. Serve hot in soup cups with a green salad for lunch, or in soup plates for a main course dish. Garnish with fresh minced parsley leaves or julienned basil, if desired.

➤ BACKGROUND INFORMATION

Wild rice isn't actually rice. Instead, it's the seed of an annual water grass found primarily in northern areas near the Great Lakes. It was a sacred food for the region's Native Americans. Native Americans still gather gourmet wild rice in their canoes, but farm-raised wild rice is cheaper and more widely available.

CHICKEN BROTH WITH KAÑIWA OR QUINOA, SPINACH,
AND EGG (STRACCIATELLA)

Chicken Broth with Kañiwa or Quinoa, Spinach, and Egg (Stracciatella)

The Italian word stracciatella *means "little shreds" or "rags," a name that reflects the appearance of the soup, as the beaten egg white forms strands once it is stirred into the hot broth. I enjoy this soup very much because it uses ingredients that are staples in many kitchens, especially the highly nourishing spinach. Over the last few years, the consumption of spinach in this country has increased to the point that spinach is now considered one of Americans' favorite vegetables. This soup is comforting and delicious, but also very quick and easy to prepare.*

YIELDS 3 SERVINGS

2 cups chicken broth

1 cup shredded spinach leaves, packed

1 egg white

1 tablespoon Parmesan cheese plus more for garnish

1 tablespoon cornstarch mixed with ¼ cup cold water

¼ teaspoon freshly ground black pepper

Dash of nutmeg

Salt (if needed, depending on broth used)

¾ cup Basic Boiled Quinoa or Basic Boiled Kañiwa, room temperature (see recipes in Chapter 1)

3 tablespoons minced fresh flat-leaf parsley leaves (optional)

1. In a 3-quart saucepan, bring chicken broth to a boil over medium heat. Add spinach and cook over low heat for 3 minutes.

2. In a small bowl, beat egg white with Parmesan cheese, cornstarch paste, black pepper, nutmeg, and salt to taste. Pour into hot broth, stirring slowly with a fork to separate the egg into strands and "rags."

3. To serve, put ¼ cup Basic Boiled Quinoa or Basic Boiled Kañiwa in a soup bowl and add a third of the soup. Garnish with parsley and with additional Parmesan cheese, if desired.

➤ VARIATIONS

This soup is similar to Chinese egg drop soup but is more nutritious. It is quick to make, but is even quicker if you buy baby spinach in plastic bags. A quick rinse, and it's ready to go. For this and other soup recipes, if you want a creamier soup, you can use amaranth in place of the quinoa or kañiwa.

LEBANESE LENTIL AND SPINACH SOUP WITH AMARANTH OR QUINOA

Lebanese Lentil and Spinach Soup with Amaranth or Quinoa

Lentil soup dates back millennia. In the Bible, it appears in the story of Esau, who renounced his birthright for a bowl of lentil soup. Fortunately, with this recipe, you don't have to do the same. Compared to other beans, lentils are easy and quick to prepare, with no overnight soaking required. There are many versions of this soup throughout the Mediterranean. This recipe was inspired by the soups I have enjoyed in Lebanese restaurants, with either Swiss chard or spinach and a few diced potatoes and small amounts of bulgur.

YIELDS ABOUT 10 1-CUP SERVINGS

2 tablespoons olive oil

2 medium onions, finely chopped (about 2 cups)

6 large cloves garlic, chopped

½ teaspoon black pepper

2 medium tomatoes (about 4 ounces each), peeled, seeded, and chopped

1 cup brown or green lentils, thoroughly washed and picked over

2 medium all-purpose potatoes, peeled and diced (½ inch)

⅓ cup raw amaranth or ⅓ cup raw quinoa, thoroughly rinsed

10 cups water

5 teaspoons chicken bouillon base

8 ounces spinach leaves, washed and coarsely chopped

¼ cup minced cilantro

¼ cup lemon juice

Salt and freshly ground black pepper to taste

Drizzle of olive oil (optional)

1. Heat oil in a large casserole over medium heat. Add onions and cook, stirring occasionally, until softened, about 5 minutes. Mash garlic and black pepper into a paste and add to casserole with the tomatoes; cook for 5 minutes, stirring.

2. Add lentils, potatoes, amaranth, water, and chicken base; bring to a boil, lower the heat, cover, and simmer for 30 minutes. Add spinach and cilantro, and continue cooking for 7 more minutes. Add lemon juice and simmer for 5 more minutes. Add salt and pepper to taste. Soup should taste tangy.

3. Serve hot in soup bowls. Drizzle olive oil to taste.

➤ VARIATIONS

You can use Swiss chard leaves instead of spinach. Wash leaves and remove ribs and coarsely chop. If a thinner soup is desired, use quinoa instead of amaranth.

MUSHROOM AND WATERCRESS SOUP WITH QUINOA

Mushroom and Watercress Soup with Quinoa

I often make this delightful soup when I want something light and nourishing. I make a practice of having 1-cup, resealable bags of cooked quinoa in the freezer to add to soups, which means I can have this ready relatively quickly. Prep time for this delicious soup can be further reduced by buying already sliced white button mushrooms. After the soup is cooked, you can chop it coarsely with a stick or immersion blender, if desired. A coarse chop makes the soup seem richer and more flavorful. This soup has good amounts of potassium, vitamins C and B_2, and niacin.

YIELDS 6–8 SERVINGS

½ cup dried porcini mushrooms

1 cup hot water

8 ounces fresh mushrooms (white, portobello, oyster, or any combination)

2 tablespoons olive oil

1 medium onion, finely chopped (about 1 cup), or you can use 1 large shallot

3 tablespoons quinoa, amaranth, or rice flour

6 cups water

4 teaspoons chicken or vegetable bouillon granules or paste

1 cup Basic Boiled Quinoa (see recipe in Chapter 1)

1 bunch watercress

3 tablespoons minced fresh flat-leaf parsley or cilantro leaves

1 small tomato (4 ounce), finely chopped (optional)

¼ teaspoon freshly grated black pepper

Juice from ½ lemon

Salt to taste

Grated Parmesan cheese (optional)

1. Soak dried mushrooms in 1 cup hot water for 30 minutes. Quickly rinse fresh mushrooms and drain well. If using oyster mushrooms, remove and discard tough stems. Chop the fresh mushrooms. Drain hydrated porcini mushrooms (strain through a fine sieve and retain soaking water), rinse well to remove particles of sand, and chop coarsely.

2. Heat oil in a 4-quart saucepan over medium heat. Add onions and mushrooms; cook, stirring, for about 5 minutes. Sprinkle flour over and cook, stirring, for a few seconds. Remove from the heat, add water from soaking mushrooms, and beat with a wooden spoon until well blended. Return to the heat, add water, bouillon cubes or granules, and Basic Boiled Quinoa, and cook, stirring, until it comes to a boil. Simmer partially covered for 10 minutes.

3. Trim tough stems from watercress and discard. Place watercress tops in a colander and wash thoroughly. Drain well and chop coarsely. Add to soup with parsley, tomato (if using), and black pepper. Cook, stirring, until watercress wilts and it is bright green. Add lemon juice, stir well, and add salt to taste.

4. Remove from heat and serve in soup bowls with Parmesan cheese on the side if desired.

QUINOA CHOWDER WITH SWISS CHARD

Quinoa Chowder with Swiss Chard

The people from the Andean countries, especially Ecuador, Peru, and Bolivia, are extremely fond of quinoa chowders, which are comfort food at its best. Chowders always have potatoes and can be made with cheese, milk, and sometimes with leafy greens, as in this case. They can be vegetarian, or they can have fish, lamb, or other meat. The sofrito used in this recipe is common to most South American countries, except that in Peru and Bolivia, ground hot peppers are added. This soup is rich in vitamin C and has good quantities of potassium, iron, calcium, and vitamins A, B_2, and B_6.

YIELDS ABOUT 10 CUPS, 1 CUP PER SERVING

2 tablespoons canola oil or butter

1 medium onion, finely chopped (about 1 cup)

4 cloves crushed garlic

1 teaspoon salt

½ teaspoon freshly ground black pepper

½ teaspoon ground cumin

½ teaspoon paprika

¼ teaspoon hot red pepper flakes

6 cups boiling water (or chicken or vegetable broth)

2 cups Basic Boiled Quinoa (see recipe in Chapter 1)

1 pound Yukon gold potatoes, peeled and cut up in 1-inch pieces

2 cups hot milk

1 cup fresh or frozen corn kernels

4 cups (abut 4 ounces) coarsely chopped Swiss chard leaves

4 ounces (1 cup packed) grated Cheddar or white cheese

Salt and freshly ground pepper to taste

2 large eggs, lightly beaten (optional)

1 Haas avocado, peeled and diced, for garnish

Minced mint, for garnish

Minced cilantro leaves, for garnish

1. In a 4-quart saucepan, melt oil or butter over low heat. Add onion and cook, stirring occasionally, for 5 minutes, without letting the onion color. Make a paste by mashing together the garlic, salt, and pepper; stir the garlic paste, cumin, paprika, and optional hot red pepper flakes in the saucepan, and cook for 1 minute. Add water or broth, Basic Boiled Quinoa, and potatoes. Simmer, partially covered, for 15 minutes or until potatoes are tender. Add milk, corn, and Swiss chard, and simmer for 5 minutes. Add cheese and cook, stirring, until cheese is melted. Add salt and pepper to taste. Stir in eggs, if desired, and cook until they have set.

2. Serve soup hot in soup plates garnished with avocado, mint, and cilantro.

➤ **BACKGROUND INFORMATION**

Sofrito originated in Spain and Portugal, where many recipes start with onion and garlic sautéed in olive oil. Spanish women moving to the Americas in the 1600s brought this cooking base with them, and sofrito become the base for most of the savory specialties in Latin America.

MANJU'S RED LENTIL SOUP WITH SQUASH AND QUINOA

Manju's Red Lentil Soup with Squash and Quinoa

Several years ago, Manju, the owner of a small Indian grocery store, gave me a recipe for a soup of red lentils, onion, potato, and salt and pepper that was cooked and then mashed or puréed. She told me it was a common comfort food where she came from in India. I loved its simplicity. That recipe became the basis for this dish, though it has evolved from a simple, puréed comfort food to a nutrition-packed soup with yellow vegetables and the added protein and fiber of quinoa.

YIELDS 8 1-CUP SERVINGS

1 winter squash, such as butternut (about 1 pound)

1 tablespoon canola oil

1 medium onion, chopped (about 1 cup)

1 clove garlic, minced

1 cup red lentils, picked and rinsed

1 cup Basic Boiled Quinoa (see recipe in Chapter 1)

5 cups hot water or vegetable or chicken broth

1 teaspoon salt (unless you use broth), plus more to taste

1 teaspoon ground turmeric

¼ teaspoon ground white pepper

Freshly ground black pepper to taste

1 hard-boiled egg, peeled and chopped

1. Wash and peel squash, and cut into large chunks.

2. In a 3- or 4-quart saucepan, heat oil over medium heat. Add onions and cook for 3 minutes or until transparent. Add garlic and stir for a few seconds. Add squash chunks, lentils, Basic Boiled Quinoa, water, salt, turmeric, and pepper. Bring to a boil, and then lower the heat, cover, and simmer for 30 minutes, adding more liquid if it dries out. By the end of this cooking time, the lentils will have fallen apart and the butternut squash will have started to break into smaller pieces. Season with salt and pepper to taste.

3. Serve in small soup bowls garnished with chopped egg.

Tomato and Onion Soup with Quinoa

This is a delicious soup I adapted from a Le Cordon Bleu recipe. In the summertime, when tomatoes are at their peak, my friends make big batches of this soup and freeze it in different size containers to enjoy summer flavors during cold winter nights. The soup provides generous amounts of vitamin C and good amounts of vitamin A.

YIELDS 6–8 SERVINGS

2 cups thinly sliced onions

2 tablespoons olive oil

1 pound tomatoes, peeled, seeded, and chopped, plus 1 tomato peeled, seeded, and julienned

2 tablespoons tomato paste

1 bay leaf

2 garlic cloves

4 cups water

4 low-sodium vegetable bouillon cubes

⅓ cup raw quinoa, thoroughly rinsed

½ teaspoon sugar

¼ teaspoon freshly ground black pepper

Coarse salt (optional), to taste

1 cup gluten-free garlic croutons

Put onions and oil in a 4-quart saucepan, cover, and cook over low heat, stirring occasionally, for 30 minutes, without letting the onions brown. Add the chopped tomatoes, tomato paste, bay leaf, and garlic; cover and simmer for 15 minutes. Add water, bouillon cubes, quinoa, sugar, pepper, and salt (if using) to taste. Bring to a boil, cover, reduce heat, and simmer, stirring occasionally, for 30 minutes. Discard bay leaf. If too thick, add more water and simmer for a few minutes more. Add the julienned tomato, bring back to a boil, and serve with croutons on the side.

Cream of Quinoa Soup

The combination of peanuts or squash seeds used in this creamy soup adds a seasoning note that, when paired with cumin and paprika, makes it a very special dish. To save time, use peanut butter or squash seed butter, which is ideal for people who are allergic to peanuts, and just mix it with the milk before adding to the soup. This soup is rich in iron and will also provide good amounts of calcium, potassium, zinc, and vitamin B$_2$ (riboflavin).

YIELDS 8 SERVINGS

1 cup raw quinoa, picked and well rinsed

4 cups water

1 tablespoon canola oil or butter

1 cup thinly sliced leek, white and light green part

1 medium onion, sliced (about 1 cup)

2 medium garlic cloves, minced

1 teaspoon paprika

½ teaspoon dry oregano, crumbled

½ teaspoon ground cumin

1 teaspoon dry mustard

1 teaspoon salt

¼ teaspoon white pepper

¼ cup peanut butter or squash seed butter

½ cup water (or chicken or vegetable bouillon)

2 cups low-fat milk, preferably organic, or soymilk, rice milk, or almond milk

1 tablespoon lemon juice

Salt and freshly ground black pepper to taste

½ cup cooked corn kernels, for garnish

½ cup grated Parmesan cheese, for garnish

Cayenne pepper or paprika, for garnish

1. In a 4- or 5-quart casserole, bring quinoa and 4 cups water to a boil over medium heat. Cook until all the water has been absorbed, about 15 minutes. Remove from the heat and set aside.

2. While quinoa is cooking, heat oil or butter in a medium-size skillet. Add leek and onion, and cook over medium-low heat, stirring occasionally until soft, about 5 minutes. Add garlic, paprika, oregano, cumin, mustard, salt, and white pepper; cook, stirring, for 1 minute. Remove from the heat and cool.

3. Add peanut butter or squash seed butter and onion mixture to a food processor and purée until smooth. Add cooked quinoa and process until puréed, adding some of the water or bouillon to thin out the thick purée.

4. Transfer quinoa purée to the casserole, add ½ cup water or bouillon and milk, and bring back to a boil over medium-low heat; cover and simmer over low heat for 5 minutes to blend flavors, stirring occasionally to avoid sticking to the bottom of casserole. If the soup is too thick, thin with additional water or milk. Add lemon juice and salt and pepper to taste.

5. Serve hot in soup bowls garnished with 1 tablespoon corn kernels, Parmesan cheese, and a dusting of cayenne pepper or paprika.

Cream of Broccoli Soup with Quinoa

In the last few years, medical newsletters and nutrition reports have been filled with praise for broccoli. It holds much promise for boosting health and preventing disease. As a result, people are trying to eat more broccoli. This soup is one example of how to use broccoli to its full advantage. It is very simple to prepare, and I can never have enough of this soup in the freezer. It is a treat for lunch or dinner.

YIELDS 8 1-CUP SERVINGS

1 tablespoon olive oil

1 cup chopped onions (about 1 medium onion)

1 cup sliced leek, white parts and 1 inch of the green

½ cup sliced celery

2 medium garlic cloves, chopped

⅓ cup raw quinoa, thoroughly rinsed

3 cups chicken or vegetable broth

4 cups water

1½ pounds broccoli

1 teaspoon dry mustard

¼ teaspoon white pepper

1 cup low-fat milk, or soymilk or almond milk

2 cups Basic Boiled Quinoa (see recipe in Chapter 1)

1 tablespoon lemon juice

Salt and pepper to taste

8 thin lemon slices or 2 tablespoons snipped chives, for garnish

½ cup sour cream mixed with 2 tablespoons heavy cream to lighten, for garnish (optional)

Croutons, for garnish (optional)

1. Heat oil in a 4-quart saucepan over medium-low heat. Add onions, leek, and celery, and cook, stirring occasionally, until they are soft, about 5 minutes. Add garlic and raw quinoa, and cook for 1 more minute. Add broth and water, bring to a boil, and simmer for 15 minutes.

2. Rinse and trim broccoli. Cut the tops (florets) from the stalks, peel the thick stalks, and cut the stalks into 1-inch pieces. Add broccoli stalks, mustard, and white pepper to the saucepan; bring to a boil and simmer for 10 minutes. Add broccoli florets and simmer for 10 more minutes. Cool for 15 minutes.

3. Purée the mixture in a blender or food processor. If using a blender, work in batches. Pass the purée through a medium sieve set over a clean saucepan. To the purée, add milk and cooked quinoa, bring back to a boil, and, if too thick, add more water, a little at a time, until you get the texture of heavy cream. Simmer for 5 minutes. Add lemon juice and salt and pepper to taste.

4. Serve soup hot in soup bowls garnished with a thin slice of lemon or snipped chives. Or drizzle the optional sour cream on each bowl and serve croutons in a separate bowl.

Cheddar Cheese and Quinoa Soup with Leeks and Chia

The quinoa-producing countries of South America have a variety of soups that are either puréed with or served with a variety of vegetables. This is a quick and excellent version of one of those creamy puréed soups. You can use any good melting cheese, but this recipe specifically calls for Cheddar because it adds to the intensity of color and flavor. From this soup, you will get good amounts of protein, calcium, iron, and vitamin B_2.

YIELDS 6 1-CUP SERVINGS

⅔ cup raw quinoa, well rinsed

1½ cups water

1 vegetable bouillon cube (optional)

1 tablespoon olive oil

1 cup sliced leeks (include 1 inch of the light green)

1 small onion, sliced (about ½ cup)

2 cloves garlic, chopped

1 teaspoon sweet paprika

½ teaspoon salt

1 teaspoon ground mustard

¼ teaspoon white ground pepper

1 cup low-fat milk, or almond milk or soymilk

1 cup grated Cheddar cheese

3 cups water (or a combination of milk and water)

Toasted Chia Seeds (see recipe in Chapter 1), for garnish

1. In a 3-quart saucepan, place quinoa with 1½ cups water and optional bouillon cube, and cook covered over medium heat for 12 minutes or until quinoa has absorbed all the water. Set aside to cool.

2. While quinoa is cooking, heat the oil in a 4-quart saucepan over medium heat. Add leek and onion and cook, stirring constantly, until transparent, about 5 minutes. Lower heat, and add garlic, paprika, salt, mustard, and pepper; cook for 10 seconds, stirring. Remove from the heat.

3. To finish the soup, combine the cooked quinoa, the leek and onion mixture, and the milk and cheese, and purée in a blender or food processor. Do this in batches if necessary.

4. Transfer purée to a clean 4-quart saucepan, add the 3 cups water (or a combination of milk and water, for a richer soup), and bring back to a boil over medium heat. Taste for salt and add more milk or water if too thick. Simmer for a couple of minutes to blend flavors. Remove from heat and serve hot in soup bowls garnished with a dusting of Toasted Chia Seeds.

SEVEN-VEGETABLE SALAD WITH QUINOA AND KAÑIWA

Seven-Vegetable Salad with Quinoa and Kañiwa

My daughter Carol eats often at an Italian restaurant close to her home, and this salad is inspired by one she loves to eat there. It is, appropriately, called Seven-Vegetable Salad. However, while the number of vegetables remains seven, the selection can change, depending on what is in season. At different times, it might have escarole, green beans, asparagus, or other vegetables—so you can vary this as desired. The addition of quinoa or kañiwa really enhances this delicious salad that is rich in vitamins C and A, folate, iron, and potassium, with good amounts of calcium and vitamins B_1, B_2, and B_6.

YIELDS 4 SERVINGS

Balsamic Dressing

½ cup extra-virgin olive oil

2 tablespoons balsamic vinegar

2 tablespoons rice wine vinegar

1 teaspoon Dijon mustard

½ teaspoon sea salt

¼ teaspoon freshly grated black pepper

Pinch sugar

Salad

2 large heirloom tomatoes, seeded and cut up in small cubes

1 medium red onion finely diced (about 1 cup) and rinsed in hot water

2 cups finely diced bell peppers (red, orange, green)

½ cup cooked corn

1 celery stalk trimmed and finely chopped (about ½ cup)

1 cup cooked white cannellini beans, drained and rinsed

2 cups any leafy greens torn in bite-size pieces

½ cup Basic Boiled Kañiwa (see recipe in Chapter 1)

½ cup Basic Boiled Quinoa (see recipe in Chapter 1; red quinoa is recommended)

1. **For Dressing:** Place the ingredients in a jar with a tight-fitting lid, and shake vigorously for a few seconds, until the mixture thickens. Shake again just before using. Refrigerate any unused dressing for up to a week.

2. **For Salad:** Place all ingredients in large bowl, and toss with ½ cup balsamic dressing. Taste and see if you need more dressing. Season with salt and pepper, if needed; divide among 4 salad plates, and serve.

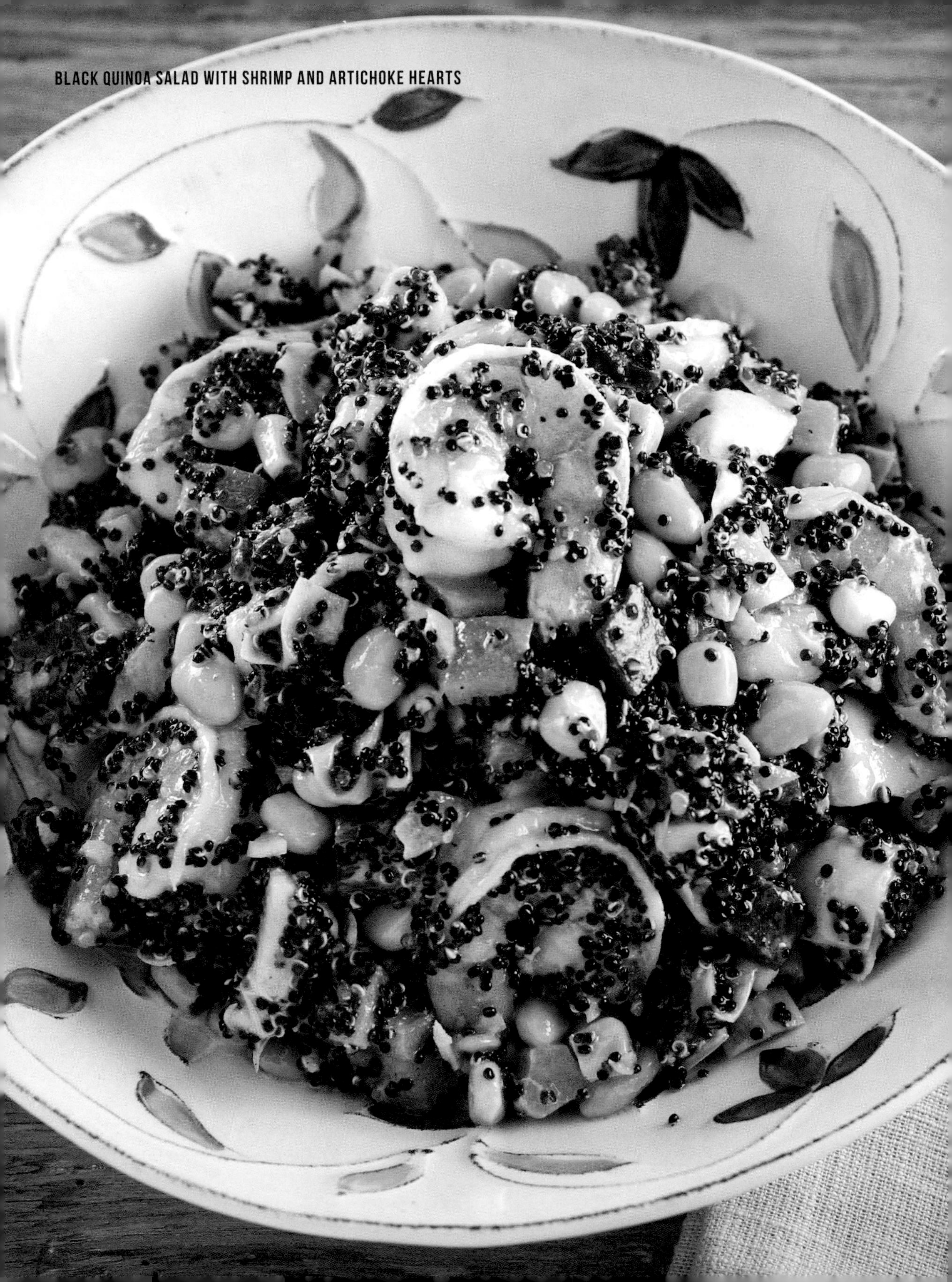

BLACK QUINOA SALAD WITH SHRIMP AND ARTICHOKE HEARTS

Black Quinoa Salad with Shrimp and Artichoke Hearts

Black quinoa is ideal for making salads and is perfect in this Black Quinoa Salad with Shrimp and Artichoke Hearts. The contrasting colors and flavors of the vegetables and shrimp found in this dish make for a very impressive-looking and delicious salad, which is packed with vitamins and rich in protein, iron, and vitamins A and C. It also has good amounts of B vitamins, zinc, and potassium. This elegant salad will enhance any table it graces.

YIELDS 8 SERVINGS

Creamy Mustard Dressing

½ cup extra-virgin olive oil

3 tablespoons sherry wine vinegar

1 tablespoon Dijon mustard

2 tablespoons whipping cream

½ teaspoon salt

½ teaspoon freshly ground black pepper

Pinch sugar

Salad

1 cup raw black quinoa

3 cloves garlic

½ teaspoon salt

¼ teaspoon freshly round black pepper

2 teaspoons fresh lemon juice

1 pound medium-size frozen shrimp, peeled and cooked (see Boiled Shrimp in Shrimp with Argentine Salsa Golf recipe in Chapter 4)

1 (14-ounce) can artichoke hearts, drained, rinsed, and cut into bite-size pieces

1 cup cooked corn kernels, drained

¾ cup frozen edamame beans, blanched in boiling salted water for 3 minutes

1 roasted red bell pepper

1 roasted yellow pepper

¼ cup fresh basil leaves torn into pieces by hand

Salt and pepper to taste

1 bunch watercress sprigs (optional)

1. **For Creamy Mustard Dressing:** Place the dressing ingredients in a jar with a tight-fitting lid, and shake vigorously for a few seconds, until the mixture is emulsified. Shake again just before using. Refrigerate any unused dressing.

2. **For Salad:** Rinse black quinoa thoroughly. Follow the recipe for Basic Boiled Quinoa in Chapter 1, but use two cups of water and cook for 20 minutes. Make a garlic paste by mashing together the garlic, salt, and pepper; mix with lemon juice. Rub the shrimp with the garlic paste. Set aside.

3. In a large salad bowl, mix together all the salad ingredients except basil, salt and pepper, and watercress; then toss the salad with half of the dressing. Refrigerate until ready to serve.

4. To serve, remove from the refrigerator 30 minutes before needed, add more dressing if needed, add basil, and toss; season with salt and pepper to taste. Transfer to a serving platter or glass bowl. This salad is colorful enough that it does not need garnishes to embellish it, but many people enjoy adding some greens, and watercress is perfect for surrounding this salad.

RED QUINOA SALAD WITH CHICKEN AND GRAPES

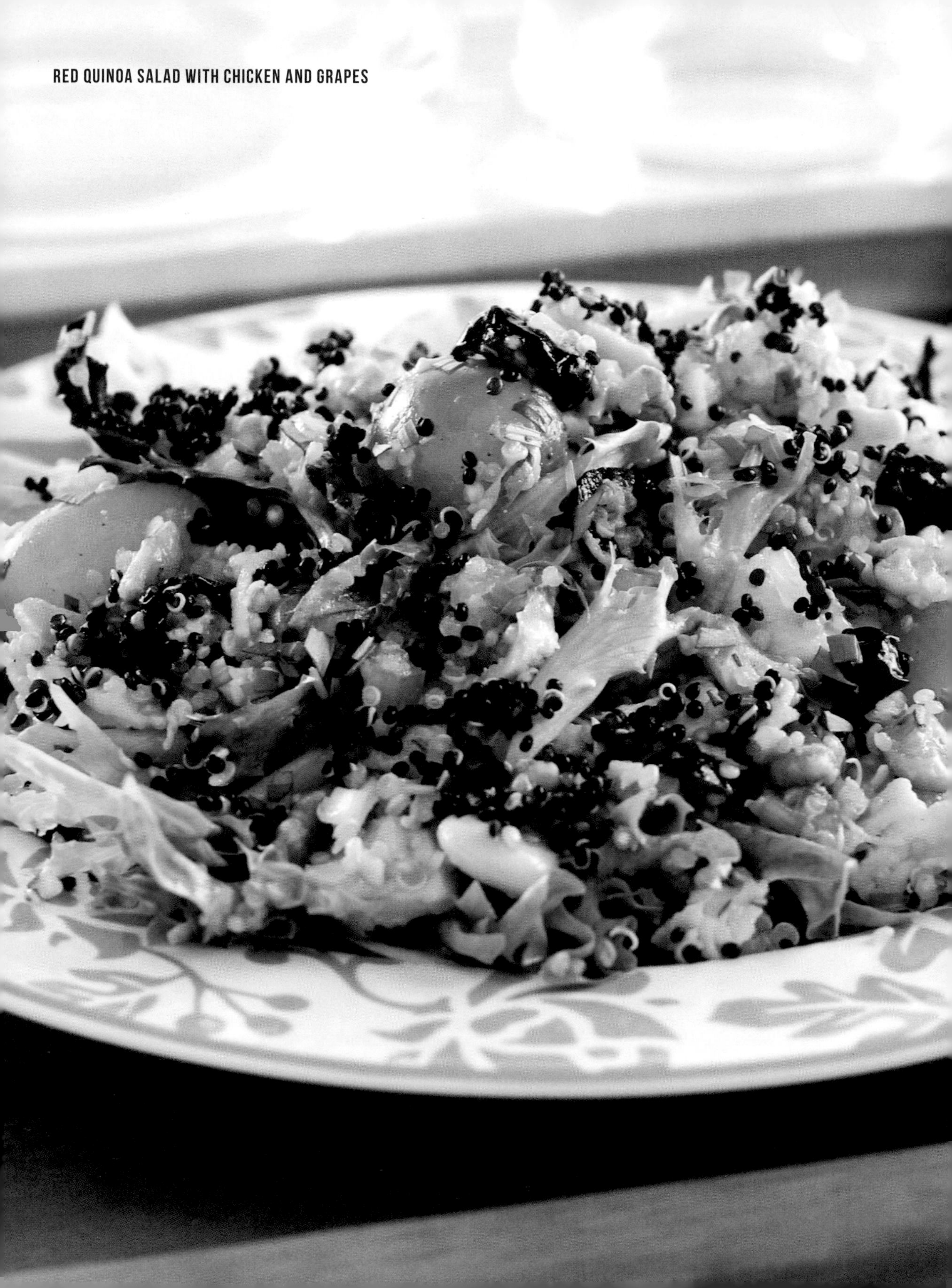

Red Quinoa Salad with Chicken and Grapes

The ingredients in this bright, refreshing, flavorful salad make it ideal for warm-weather luncheons. The grapes used in this dish are a classic addition to chicken salad. They add interest but also a touch of sweetness that perfectly balances the other elements. Tarragon is optional, but you may find that its hint of licorice flavor goes well with the sweetness offered by the grapes.

YIELDS 6 SERVINGS

¾ cup Basic Boiled Quinoa (see recipe in Chapter 1; red quinoa recommended)

2 cups diced (¼ inch) cooked chicken breast

½ cup finely diced white onion

1 cup finely diced celery

1 bunch curly endive

1 cup small seedless green grapes

½ cup dried cranberries

½ cup lupini beans, skins removed

½ cup coarsely chopped walnuts

¼ cup minced fresh parsley

1–2 tablespoons fresh tarragon leaves (optional)

1 batch Creamy Mustard Dressing (see recipe for Black Quinoa Salad with Shrimp and Artichoke Hearts in this chapter)

Salt and pepper to taste

1. In a large salad bowl, combine Basic Boiled Quinoa, chicken, onions, and celery. This can be done a few hours ahead, covered, and refrigerated until needed.

2. Remove curly parts from the endive and rinse well. Dry and keep in a plastic container until needed.

3. Just before serving, combine chicken and quinoa mixture with grapes, cranberries, lupini beans, walnuts, herbs, and endive curls. Add Creamy Mustard Dressing, and toss salad. Taste and add salt and pepper if needed.

Quinoa Salad with Beluga Lentils and Shrimp

In this amazing salad, hearts of palm, a favorite of Latin Americans, blends beautifully with the rest of the ingredients like the beluga lentils, which are fast to cook and can sometimes be found canned. If you can't find beluga lentils, you can substitute with any kind of lentils. This salad, which is rich in iron and folate, and also has good amounts of vitamins C, B$_6$, and B$_1$, as well as niacin, potassium, and zinc, is also great if made with cooked turkey breast.

YIELDS ABOUT 6 CUPS, 1 CUP PER SERVING

Sherry Mustard Vinaigrette

¼ cup extra-virgin olive oil

2 tablespoons canola oil

3 tablespoons sherry vinegar

1 tablespoon stone-ground Dijon mustard

½ teaspoon salt

½ teaspoon freshly ground black pepper

⅓ teaspoon sugar

Salad

1 cup beluga lentils

1 cup cooked salad shrimp

2 cups Basic Boiled Quinoa (see recipe in Chapter 1)

1 cup cooked or canned white corn kernels

⅓ cup each diced (¼ inch) red, orange, and green bell peppers

½ cup chopped Vidalia or other sweet, white onions

2 large garlic cloves, minced

1 batch Sherry Mustard Vinaigrette

2 tablespoons chopped fresh parsley

2 tablespoons cilantro leaves or fresh basil leaves

8 cherry tomatoes, halved, or tomato wedges, for garnish

2 tablespoons Toasted Chia Seeds (see recipe in Chapter 1), for garnish

1. **For Sherry Mustard Vinaigrette:** In a small bowl, beat oils with vinegar, mustard, salt, pepper, and sugar until emulsified.

2. **For Salad:** Cook lentils according to package directions. Drain and rinse. In a mixing bowl, combine shrimp with Basic Boiled Quinoa, lentils, corn, peppers, onion, and garlic. Toss salad with ½ batch of vinaigrette, taste to see if more salt is needed, cover, and refrigerate until needed.

3. Just before serving, toss salad with parsley and cilantro or basil, add more of the vinaigrette to taste, transfer to a serving bowl, and garnish with tomatoes and Toasted Chia Seeds.

Quinoa, Black Rice, and Smoked Salmon Salad

Everywhere I go, I get ideas for salads. I ate a salad similar to this one at the College of Lake County in northern Illinois, where the culinary students prepare excellent lunches. Their salad was made with wild rice, salmon, pecans, and other ingredients. Inspired by this, I decided to make something using quinoa and black rice instead of wild rice. This very colorful and delicious salad is rich in vitamin C and also offers good amounts of vitamin A, the B vitamins, potassium, iron, and zinc.

YIELDS 6 SERVINGS

Maple Dressing

½ cup extra-virgin olive oil

¼ cup canola oil

2 tablespoons coconut vinegar

2 tablespoons lemon juice

1 tablespoon maple syrup

¼ teaspoon sea salt

½ teaspoon freshly ground black pepper

Salad

2 cups Basic Boiled Quinoa (see recipe in Chapter 1; white quinoa recommended)

1 cup cooked black rice (cook according to package directions)

6 ounces smoked salmon, broken into small pieces

½ cup sliced (1/16-inch thick) radishes

¼ cup thinly sliced shallots

¾ cup coarsely chopped sweet, white onions, preferably Vidalia

½ cup lightly toasted pecans

¼ cup finely diced yellow pepper

½ (14-ounce) can hearts of palm, drained, split lengthwise, and sliced in ½-inch half-moons

¼ cup dried cherries or cranberries

4 cups curly endive cut up into bite-size pieces, rinsed, and dried

½ cup Maple Dressing

1. **For Maple Dressing:** Place dressing ingredients in a jar with a tight-fitting lid and shake vigorously for a few seconds, until emulsified. Set aside or refrigerate for up to 1 week.

2. **For Salad:** Toss all salad ingredients in a large bowl, drizzle with Maple Dressing, and gently toss salad. Divide among 6 salad plates and serve immediately. Note: If you're preparing this dish ahead of time, store the ingredients in separate containers. The black rice and radishes bleed when in touch with other ingredients, so it is better to keep separate until ready to serve.

➤ BACKGROUND INFORMATION

Black rice, also known as Emperors' rice, purple rice, or forbidden rice, is a fragrant, exceptionally nutritious rice that is highly valued in Asia. It is often available at major supermarkets. Otherwise, you can visit an Asian grocery store or search for it online at Amazon (www.amazon.com).

QUINOA SALAD WITH CORN AND BLACK BEANS

Quinoa Salad with Corn and Black Beans

A version of this salad first appeared in my booklet, The Art of Cooking with Quinoa. *This bright, colorful salad has been praised, even by people who were unfamiliar with quinoa. It is appealing to the eye as well as the appetite, and it is substantial enough to serve as a main course. This version includes chicken, and the breast from a rotisserie chicken is ideal for this type of salad, but it is also wonderful with shrimp. However, chicken is optional, and I include instructions for how to make it vegetarian. This salad provides high amounts of vitamin C, in addition to good amounts of iron, protein, and fiber.*

YIELDS 8–10 SERVINGS

3 cups Basic Boiled Quinoa (see recipe in Chapter 1)

1½ cups cooked chicken, diced ¼ inch (optional)

1 (15.5-ounce) can black beans, drained and rinsed

1 cup cooked fresh or frozen white corn kernels, drained

½ cup seeded and diced (¼ inch) red bell pepper

½ cup seeded and diced (¼ inch) green bell pepper

½ cup chopped red onions, rinsed with hot water and patted dry

¼ cup thinly sliced scallions (white part and 1 inch of the green)

1 batch Sherry Mustard Vinaigrette (see Quinoa Salad with Beluga Lentils and Shrimp recipe in this chapter)

¼ cup minced fresh cilantro, parsley, or basil leaves

Greens such as baby arugula or spinach, coarsely chopped, for garnish

¼ cup lightly toasted slivered almonds, for garnish

Cherry tomatoes, halved, for garnish

1. Place Basic Boiled Quinoa in a large mixing bowl to cool. Add chicken (if using), beans, corn, bell peppers, onions, and scallions; toss to combine well.

2. Toss the salad with half of the Sherry Mustard Vinaigrette (use a little less for vegetarian version). Taste to see if more salt is needed. Cover and refrigerate until needed.

3. Just before serving, taste again, and add more Sherry Mustard Vinaigrette if needed. Toss with the cilantro and serve on a bed of greens drizzled with a tablespoon of Sherry Mustard Vinaigrette. Garnish with almonds and halved cherry tomatoes.

QUINOA, POTATO, AND NOVA SALMON SALAD

Quinoa, Potato, and Nova Salmon Salad

This recipe was inspired by a a salad enjoyed in the countries of the Andes, where the potato originated. It is a very versatile salad that goes well with a wide range of proteins, such as cooked chicken, turkey, or shrimp. However, it is especially colorful with the Nova salmon. This salad is rich in vitamins C and A, and has good amounts of potassium, iron, vitamins B_1 and B_6, folate, and niacin.

YIELDS ABOUT 6 CUPS, 1 CUP PER SERVING

Creamy Herb Dressing

⅓ cup extra-virgin olive oil

2 tablespoons white wine vinegar

2 tablespoons heavy cream

1 tablespoon fresh lemon juice

1 teaspoon coarse mustard

½ teaspoon sea salt

¼ teaspoon freshly ground black pepper

Pinch sugar

¼ cup minced fresh parsley or cilantro leaves

1–2 tablespoons fresh-snipped chives

Salad

2 cups Basic Boiled Quinoa (see recipe in Chapter 1)

8 ounces Nova salmon, cut into 1-inch pieces

1½ cups cooked diced (½ inch) potatoes

1½ cups cooked frozen carrots and peas cooked al dente

¾ cup julienned (½ inch) white onion

1 cup finely diced celery

½ cup lupini beans, skins removed

8 Greek black olives, pitted and halved

Salt and pepper to taste

1 head Boston lettuce

1. **For Creamy Herb Dressing:** Place all dressing ingredients except herbs in a jar with a tight-fitting lid and shake vigorously for a few seconds, until emulsified. Set aside or refrigerate until needed. Add herbs just before using, and refrigerate any unused dressing for up to 1 week.

2. **For Salad:** In a large salad bowl, combine Basic Boiled Quinoa, salmon, potatoes, carrots and peas, onions, celery, and lupini beans. This can be done a few hours ahead, covered, and refrigerated until needed.

3. Just before serving, add olives. Add herbs to dressing, shake dressing well, and add to salad. Toss salad. Taste and add salt and pepper if needed.

4. To serve, arrange Boston lettuce leaves around a serving platter and mound salad in the center of platter. This salad is so colorful, it does not need to be garnished.

ARUGULA AND RADICCHIO SALAD WITH GOAT CHEESE

Arugula and Radicchio Salad with Goat Cheese

This salad is great if you love goat cheese—and even if you don't. I know a few people who don't, so I give the option of using feta cheese, which is a good substitute. This salad is rich in vitamins A, C, and B$_2$, as well as calcium and iron. It also has good amounts of potassium and zinc.

YIELDS 4 SERVINGS

Mustard Honey Dressing

¼ cup extra-virgin olive oil

2 tablespoons canola oil

3 tablespoons fresh lime juice

1 tablespoon Dijon mustard

2 tablespoons honey

½ teaspoon sea salt

¼ teaspoon freshly ground black pepper

Salad

4 cups baby arugula or watercress

2 cups radicchio, cleaned and shredded

1 cup green grapes

4 ounces goat cheese or feta cheese

1 cup Basic Boiled Quinoa (see recipe in Chapter 1; white quinoa recommended)

1 batch Mustard Honey Dressing

½ cup toasted pine nuts

1. **For Mustard Honey Dressing:** Put all ingredients in a jar with a tight-fitting lid and shake until emulsified. Or, for a creamier version, put all ingredients in a blender and process for a few seconds. Chill until needed.

2. **For Salad:** Place arugula and shredded radicchio in a large bowl of cold water with ice and let it stand for 2 hours. Drain and dry in a salad spinner. Place in a plastic bag or plastic container lined with paper towels; cover and keep in refrigerator until needed.

3. Clean grapes and store in a covered plastic container. Slice cheese in 8 rounds (or crumble feta cheese).

4. To serve, mix arugula, radicchio, Basic Boiled Quinoa, and grapes in a mixing bowl. Toss with Mustard Honey Dressing to taste, divide among 4 salad plates, arrange 2 cheese slices on top or, if using feta cheese, top with crumbled feta cheese, and sprinkle with pine nuts.

Roasted Beets with Fresh Mozzarella Balls

Roasted beets are delicious; the roasting seems to intensify the sweetness and deepens the flavor. Now you can find beets of different colors, which make colorful salads. When buying beets, try to get them in a bunch with the greens still attached. The beets should be firm to the touch, and the greens should be bright and fresh.

YIELDS 4 SERVINGS

4 medium-size beets

4 small fresh mozzarella balls

1 bunch watercress, trimmed, washed, dried

1 cup Basic Boiled Quinoa (see recipe in Chapter 1; tricolor or
    rainbow quinoa is recommended)

½ cup toasted, coarsely chopped hazelnuts

½ cup Creamy Mustard Dressing (see recipe for Black Quinoa
    Salad with Shrimp and Artichoke Hearts in this chapter)

1. Preheat the oven to 400°F. Cut the greens off the beets, leaving ½-inch stems. Reserve greens for another use. Wash beets carefully, wrap in aluminum foil, and bake for 45 minutes or more, depending on the size. (To test for doneness, use a paring knife—if the beet is done, the knife should go into the beet easily.) Cool, peel, and slice about ⅛-inch thick; then cut mozzarella balls in ¼-inch rounds.

2. To serve, divide watercress among 4 plates. Top each salad with ¼ cup Basic Boiled Quinoa. Arrange beets around border of quinoa, alternating with cheese. Sprinkle hazelnuts on top. Drizzle with Creamy Mustard Dressing and serve right away.

Mixed Greens with Froggy's Creamy French Dressing

Froggy's French Restaurant (www.froggysrestaurant.com), a venerable and much-loved restaurant in Highwood, Illinois, is one of my favorite places for lunch or dinner with friends. The restaurant offers a wonderful range of country French cuisine, and I love their bright, flavorful, creamy French salad dressing that they were kind enough to share with me. To overcome the concern about possible problems with raw eggs, the chef at Froggy's lets the egg sit in the vinegar for half an hour. If you can find pasteurized eggs at your market, use them, to feel safe.

YIELDS 4 SERVINGS

Froggy's Creamy French Dressing

½ cup wine vinegar, red or white

1 large egg

1 tablespoon Dijon mustard

½ teaspoon salt

¼ teaspoon freshly ground black pepper

1 cup grape seed oil

Salad

4 cups mixed greens

1 cup Basic Boiled Quinoa (see recipe in Chapter 1)

½ cup julienned raw beets (optional)

½ cup julienned raw carrots (optional)

½ cup Marcona almonds

1 batch Froggy's Creamy French Dressing

1. **For Froggy's Creamy French Dressing:** Place vinegar in a small bowl. Break the egg into the vinegar and let stand for 10 minutes; then beat the egg and vinegar until well mixed. Add Dijon mustard, salt, and pepper, and beat until well incorporated. Add oil and beat with a wire whisk until creamy or process in a blender until smooth. Use immediately or put in a glass jar and refrigerate.

2. **For Salad:** Place 1 cup greens on each of 4 salad plates. Toss Basic Boiled Quinoa, beets, and carrots together (if using beets and carrots). Divide into four portions and mound on top of greens. Scatter 2 tablespoons almonds over each salad, drizzle each with 2 tablespoons Froggy's Creamy French Dressing, and serve.

➤ VARIATIONS

The salads at Froggy's always have a variety of salad greens, mostly the more delicate Boston or Bibb lettuces, or lettuce leaves of different colors. Use what you prefer, but take advantage of the variety of greens that are offered in the supermarkets, and, if you have the time, add color by adding julienne of carrots or beets like they do at Froggy's.

CHAPTER 6
Entrées

Throughout the ages, the main meal of the day has been the magnet to draw people together, whether it was around the fire or around the table. Main courses are the most important part of these meals, and are often the only part, whether for economic reasons or because of time constraints. Many of the recipes found in this chapter are one-pot meals that are traditional, delicious, and designed to make your busy life easier. I hope they once again draw families and friends to the table.

Many of the quinoa and amaranth dishes I feature in this book were adapted from the Amerindian larder. The indigenous people relied on one-pot cooking largely because one pot was, for much of history, the only cooking vessel available. They prepared their meals in big clay pots, using indigenous foods such as corn, beans, potatoes, sweet potatoes, and green leafy vegetables, along with quinoa, amaranth, or kañiwa. Even now, with more sophisticated equipment available, one-pot meals are a great way to stretch small amounts of meat, an important consideration for those who are trying to reduce their meat intake. In fact, some of the one-pot meals can be served without meat and will still be delicious and nutritious, thanks to the use of the ancient super grains. By adding some vegetables and other hearty, filling ingredients, such as potatoes, legumes, and rice or pasta, you can feed a large family economically and wholesomely—but also splendidly. The delicious dishes found in this chapter may very well become family favorites. Enjoy.

RED QUINOA RISOTTO WITH PORCINI MUSHROOMS

Red Quinoa Risotto with Porcini Mushrooms

Quinoa is a great alternative to rice, so it wasn't a surprise to me when, on my last trip to Argentina, I found quinoa risotto. When I made it, the only problem I found was that quinoa does not have the starch that gives the creamy texture to risotto like risotto rices (such as arborio or carnaroli) do. I decided to add some rice flour to make up for the lack of starch in quinoa. As an alternative, you can do as the French do and add a few spoonfuls of cream instead.

YIELDS 4 SERVINGS

½ cup dried porcini mushrooms, soaked in hot water for 30 minutes

2 cups water

1 cup raw red quinoa, well rinsed

1 tablespoon canola oil

1 tablespooon unsalted butter

1 cup minced onion

2 garlic cloves, passed through a garlic press

¼ teaspoon freshly ground black pepper

2 teaspoons rice flour (optional)

½ cup dry white wine

2–3 cups chicken or vegetable broth

¾ cup cooked sweet corn

1 small roasted poblano or green chili pepper, homemade or canned, seeded, peeled, and chopped

Salt to taste

½ cup shredded fontina cheese

¼ cup shaved Parmesan cheese, preferably Parmigiano-Reggiano

12 large Spiced Shrimp (see Shrimp with Argentine Salsa Golf recipe in Chapter 4) (optional)

1. Drain mushrooms; rinse them well rubbing off sand with fingers. Chop in small pieces and set aside.

2. In a 4-quart saucepan, bring water and quinoa to a boil over medium heat and cook until quinoa has absorbed all the water, about 15 minutes.

3. While quinoa is cooking, heat oil and butter in a medium-size skillet, and cook onion and mushrooms over medium heat for 5 minutes or until onion is softened. Stir in garlic, black pepper, and optional rice flour, and cook, stirring, for 2 minutes, to blend flavors. Add onion and mushroom mixture to the quinoa. Stir in wine and cook over medium heat until wine is absorbed, about 10 minutes.

4. Bring the chicken or vegetable broth to a simmer over medium heat, then reduce to low. Add 2 cups simmering broth to quinoa. Cook quinoa over medium-high heat, stirring constantly, until most of the broth is absorbed, about 15 minutes. Add corn and poblano pepper, and mix well. The consistency of the quinoa at this point should be almost soupy, with the germ/halos separated from the grain. If too dry, add ½ cup more broth. Season with salt to taste.

5. Stir in fontina cheese, and then sprinkle shaved Parmesan cheese on top. Garnish with shrimp, if desired. Serve immediately.

Soupy Puerto Rican Quinoa with Chicken

I originally developed this recipe for FamilyFun magazine. The editor wanted a quinoa dish that would be moist and flavorful, and I thought of a Puerto Rican specialty traditionally made with rice and chicken. The name of this recipe comes from the Spanish sopa *(soup) and refers to the soupy consistency of the dish at the moment it is taken off the heat. As it sits, the quinoa absorbs all the liquid, so it doesn't stay soupy—but it does produce a beautifully moist dish.*

YIELDS 4–6 SERVINGS

6 skinless chicken parts (2 breast halves, 2 legs, 2 thighs)

1 teaspoon salt

½ teaspoon crumbled, dried oregano

¼ teaspoon freshly ground black pepper

2 cloves garlic, passed through a garlic press

2 tablespoons finely chopped fresh cilantro leaves

3 tablespoons canola oil, divided

1 teaspoon ground sweet paprika or annatto powder

1 (4-ounce) piece cooked ham, cut into ¼-inch dice (about 1 cup)

1 medium onion, finely chopped (about 1 cup)

1 small green bell pepper, cored and finely chopped (about 1 cup)

1 tablespoon white vinegar

½ cup tomato sauce

1 tablespoon small capers

½ cup sliced Spanish olives

3 cups chicken broth, hot

Salt and pepper to taste

1 cup raw quinoa, thoroughly rinsed

½ cup cooked peas, for garnish

1 roasted red pepper, sliced into thin strips, for garnish

Grated Parmesan cheese to taste, for garnish

1. Remove fat and gristle from chicken parts. Cut each breast half in half, across (to make it roughly the same size as the legs and thighs). In a small bowl, mix salt with oregano, black pepper, garlic, cilantro, and 1 tablespoon oil. (Salt can be left out if it is an issue for you.) Rub chicken parts with this mixture, and place in a bowl to marinate in the refrigerator for 30 minutes.

2. In a 5- to 6-quart Dutch oven, preferably nonstick, heat remaining 2 tablespoons oil over medium heat. Stir in paprika or annatto powder, ham, onion, and bell pepper, and sauté, stirring occasionally, until onion is transparent, about 5 minutes. Add vinegar, tomato sauce, capers, and olives; mix well, and cook for 2 minutes. Add chicken pieces, turning them around to coat with onion mixture. Cover and cook until chicken is done, turning pieces occasionally, about 25 more minutes, depending on size of pieces.

3. Add chicken broth, mix well, and bring to a boil; add salt and pepper to taste, stir in quinoa, and continue cooking, uncovered, until quinoa is transparent throughout, about 15 minutes. Remove from the heat; it will be soupy but will continue cooking and absorbing the liquid, just like risotto. Can be served immediately, but you can also wait until the quinoa has absorbed most of the liquid. Ladle into soup bowls and garnish with peas, roasted red pepper, and a sprinkle of Parmesan cheese, to taste.

➤ VARIATIONS

Many people feel this dish tastes even better the next day, but don't garnish until you are ready to eat it. Refrigerate overnight; then reheat, garnish, and enjoy.

Quinoa Casserole with Meat and Vegetables

In the quinoa-producing countries of Ecuador, Peru, and Bolivia, locals make wonderful one-pot meals, like this one. This casserole is traditionally made with pork, but beef can easily be substituted, and it can even be made without meat. This dish is not only rich in B vitamins but also in vitamins A and C, plus iron, zinc, potassium, and good amounts of calcium. The only thing this splendid dish needs to make a complete meal is a refreshing salad made with avocado and arugula or other green lettuces.

YIELDS ABOUT 6 PINTS, OR 6–8 SERVINGS

1 tablespoon canola oil

1 cup finely chopped leek, white part with some of the light green (about 1 large)

1 medium onion, finely chopped (about 1 cup)

4 medium cloves garlic, minced

1 teaspoon sweet paprika

½ teaspoon ground cumin

1 teaspoon salt

½ teaspoon freshly ground black pepper

¼ teaspoon red pepper flakes

12 ounces pork shoulder (or beef chuck), excess fat removed and cut up into ¾-inch dice

8 cups hot water (or vegetable broth, if not using meat), divided

1 cup raw quinoa, well rinsed

4 large cabbage leaves, rinsed and cut up into 1-inch dice (about 2 cups, pressed down)

2 medium carrots, peeled and cut into 1-inch slices

1 pound yellow potatoes, peeled and cut into 1-inch pieces

½ cup peeled squash seeds (pepitas), lightly toasted, or peanut butter

½ cup milk

1 cup frozen peas or edamame beans

Salt and pepper to taste

¼ cup minced fresh parsley leaves or cilantro leaves

1. Heat oil in a heavy casserole over low heat. Add leeks and onions and cook, stirring occasionally, for 5 minutes, until softened. Add garlic, paprika, cumin, salt, black pepper, and red pepper flakes, and cook, stirring, for 30 seconds. Increase the heat to medium, add meat, and toss until well coated with the onion mixture and lightly browned, about 5 minutes. Add 2 cups water and bring to a boil. Reduce the heat to low and simmer for 30 minutes. Add remaining hot water or broth and bring to a boil.

2. Add quinoa, cabbage, carrots, and potatoes; partially cover and continue to cook, stirring occasionally, until potatoes are tender, about 20 minutes.

3. In a blender, purée the seeds and the milk. (If using peanut butter, use the blender to combine it with the milk.) Add to the casserole with peas or edamame beans. (Edamame beans are higher in protein than peas, so are a better choice if you are not using meat.) Stir until well blended and simmer for 5 minutes. Add more water or broth if stew is too thick. Sauce should be medium thick. Add salt and pepper to taste and serve hot in soup bowls garnished with cilantro or parsley.

➤ BACKGROUND INFORMATION

Many Americans, when they hear the word "casserole," think of a specific type of food rather than a type of cookware. The word refers to a deep dish in which food can be baked and served. In time, food cooked in a casserole also became known as a casserole.

QUINOA CASSEROLE WITH MEAT AND VEGETABLES

Quinoa with Chicken Sausage and Hearts of Palm

A Spanish paella-like rice dish inspired this recipe, which uses quinoa instead of rice. Dishes of this type are complete meals and can be a powerhouse of nutrition. This dish is rich in vitamins C and A, as well as potassium, zinc, and iron, and it also has good amounts of most of the B vitamins. And it's delicious, too.

YIELDS ABOUT 8 CUPS, 1 CUP PER SERVING

8 ounces organic chicken sausage, plain or flavored with spices, such as chorizo style

2 tablespoons olive oil

1 medium red onion, finely chopped (about 1 cup)

¾ cup diced green bell pepper

4 cloves garlic, chopped and put through a garlic press

½ teaspoon salt

¼ teaspoon freshly ground black pepper

2 tablespoons finely chopped fresh parsley leaves

1 cup raw quinoa, thoroughly rinsed

⅓ cup seedless black raisins (optional)

2 cups hot vegetable broth or water

½ teaspoon crumbled saffron threads

2 teaspoons sweet paprika, preferably Spanish

1 (14-ounce) can chickpeas, drained and rinsed

1 (14-ounce) can chopped hearts of palm, drained, rinsed, and cut into smaller pieces if too large

¼ cup red pimento strips, homemade or bottled

1 hard-boiled egg, shelled and cut into thin wedges

8 pitted black olives

1. Remove casing from sausage; slice into ½-inch rounds. Heat a 4-quart casserole dish, preferably nonstick, over medium heat. Add sliced sausage and brown on both sides until lightly colored, about 5 minutes. Remove and reserve.

2. To casserole dish, add the oil, onion, and bell pepper; cook, stirring occasionally, for about 5 minutes or until onion has softened. Add garlic, salt, black pepper, and parsley, and cook, while stirring, for 1 minute. Add quinoa and continue cooking for 1 minute, stirring until all grains are coated with the oil. Add the raisins, if desired. In a separate bowl, combine the vegetable broth, saffron threads, and sweet paprika. Add broth mixture to the casserole dish and bring to a boil. Reduce the heat to low, and cook covered until the quinoa absorbs most of the liquid and forms wells on the surface, about 10 minutes.

3. Add reserved sausage, chickpeas, hearts of palm, and pimento, pressing down a little into the quinoa; cover and continue cooking for 5 more minutes. Remove from the heat, fluff with a fork, cover with a kitchen towel and the cover on top, and let it sit to dry until needed. Fluff and serve garnished with sliced egg and black olives.

➤ VARIATIONS

Chicken sausages are found in a variety of flavors, such as the classic chorizo, Mexican, Italian, bratwurst, or hot dogs, and many of them are made from soy, which are ideal for vegetarians. Any one of them can be used for this dish. These sausages need very little cooking.

Bell Peppers Stuffed with Amaranth/Quinoa and Turkey

When it comes to stuffed vegetables, bell peppers are a crowd pleaser because they lend themselves to a wide variety of fillings and flavors. They can be served with or without a sauce, and the stuffing can be made vegetarian by omitting the turkey and adding some pine nuts and raisins. This recipe is my own creation, though it is anchored in tradition. Instead of the more common rice filling, I have used amaranth. Rarely will you find a dish that is so rich in all the essential vitamins for good health, especially vitamins C and A, the B vitamins, plus iron.

YIELDS 4 SERVINGS

4 medium bell peppers, green, red, or orange

8 cups water

2 tablespoons olive oil

1 small onion, chopped (about ½ cup)

2 cloves garlic, minced, or ½ teaspoon granulated garlic

8 ounces ground turkey (or chicken), preferably organic

½ teaspoon sweet paprika

¼ teaspoon dried red pepper flakes, or to taste

½ teaspoon salt

¼ teaspoon ground cumin

¼ teaspoon ground allspice

¼ teaspoon freshly ground black pepper

1 teaspoon Worcestershire sauce

1½ cups Basic Boiled Amaranth or Basic Boiled Quinoa (see recipes in Chapter 1)

½ cup cooked peas

¼ cup lightly toasted pine nuts

¼ cup finely chopped fresh parsley leaves

1 large egg, lightly beaten

2 cups canned tomato sauce, divided

¼ cup grated Parmesan or manchego cheese (optional)

1. Cut off tops of the peppers, and remove seeds. Bring 8 cups water to a boil in a 4-quart saucepan. Drop peppers in and cook for 5 minutes. Drain well and set aside.

2. Heat oil in a large skillet over medium heat. Add onion and cook, stirring, until softened, about 3 minutes. Stir in garlic and ground turkey or chicken, and cook, breaking up meat and stirring, until meat loses its pink color. Add paprika, red pepper flakes, salt, cumin, allspice, black pepper, and Worcestershire sauce; stir well and cook for 1 minute to blend flavors.

3. Transfer turkey to a mixing bowl, mix thoroughly with Basic Boiled Amaranth or Basic Boiled Quinoa, peas, pine nuts, parsley, egg, and ½ cup tomato sauce. Taste and add salt if needed.

4. Divide the turkey/amaranth or quinoa mixture into 4 portions and fill each pepper with the mixture. Stand stuffed peppers upright in a shallow, greased, 9-inch baking dish. Cover with the rest of the sauce, and sprinkle with optional Parmesan. Peppers can be prepared ahead to this point. If not being cooked immediately, cool, cover, and refrigerate until needed.

5. One hour before serving, bring peppers to room temperature. Preheat the oven to 375°F. Cover with foil and bake for 30 minutes. Remove the foil, spoon over some of the sauce, and cook for an additional 10 minutes, or until peppers are beginning to collapse. Serve peppers with some of the sauce left in the baking dish and mashed potatoes. A green salad with a vinaigrette dressing rounds out the meal.

➤ KITCHEN WISDOM

If you want to freeze the peppers for later use, bake them for only 30 minutes. Let them cool to room temperature, wrap, and freeze. Then, when ready to serve, defrost the peppers overnight in the refrigerator and bake in a preheated 350°F oven for 20 minutes or until tender.

BELL PEPPERS STUFFED WITH AMARANTH/QUINOA AND TURKEY

Easy Black Beans with Quinoa, Chia Seeds, and Artichoke Hearts

Black bean dishes are staples in many Latin American countries, and this version is especially good because the artichoke hearts provide a nice contrast to the beans and add powerful nutrients. This is a great way to introduce quinoa to children or others who might resist something new, as the black beans color the dish so thoroughly that the quinoa will hardly be visible. You'll be pleased to know that this dish is rich in folate; vitamins C, B_1, and B_6; potassium; and iron. It also has good amounts of calcium, zinc, vitamins A and B_2, and niacin.

YIELDS 4 SERVINGS

2 tablespoons olive oil

1 medium onion, finely chopped (about 1 cup)

½ cup chopped green or red bell pepper

3 cloves garlic, passed through a garlic press

2 tablespoons tomato paste

½ teaspoon ground cumin

1 teaspoon dried oregano, crumbled

½ teaspoon freshly ground black pepper

3 or 4 canned or frozen artichoke hearts, rinsed and cut into bite-size pieces

1 cup Basic Boiled Quinoa (see recipe in Chapter 1)

1 (30-ounce) can black beans (or 4 cups homemade, liquid included)

1 can water (use empty bean can)

Salt to taste

1 tablespoon cider vinegar

4 cups of cooked white or brown rice (optional)

¼ cup Toasted Chia Seeds, for garnish (see recipe in Chapter 1)

1. In a 2-quart saucepan, heat oil over medium heat. Add onions and peppers, and cook, stirring occasionally, until soft, about 4–5 minutes. Add garlic and cook, stirring, for 10 seconds.

2. Stir in tomato paste, cumin, oregano, and black pepper, and cook for 1 minute. Toss in artichokes, Basic Boiled Quinoa, black beans, and water. Bring to a boil, and then lower heat and simmer, partially covered and stirring occasionally, until sauce has thickened, about 20 minutes. Add salt to taste. (Depending on how salty the beans are, you might not need to add any more salt.) Stir in vinegar, serve over rice, and garnish with Toasted Chia Seeds.

➤ VARIATIONS

Any color quinoa works in this recipe, but if you have black quinoa, the color blends even more completely, creating a greater contrast with the rice. Keep in mind that the beans can be eaten alone but are more traditional if served over rice (brown or white). Serving over quinoa is another nutritious option. While this is often a main course, it also makes a good side dish with meat of some sort.

QUINOA POLENTA WITH CREAMED MUSHROOMS

Quinoa Polenta with Creamed Mushrooms

My daughter Patty is a busy professional who eats healthy meals and loves comfort foods. This is one of her favorite dishes for a quick meal. Buy presliced mushrooms that look perfectly white and firm. It saves time, as all they need is a quick rinse. You can add dried mushrooms for extra taste, or use different types of fresh mushrooms, such as shiitake or portobello. This dish is not only rich in protein, vitamin B_2, and niacin, but it also has good amounts of potassium, calcium, iron, vitamin A, and folate.

YIELDS 4 SERVINGS

Polenta

3 cups water

½ teaspoon salt

1 bay leaf

1 bruised garlic clove

½ cup instant polenta

1 cup Basic Boiled Quinoa (see recipe in Chapter 1)

⅓ cup grated Parmesan or manchego cheese

Salt and pepper to taste

Creamed Mushrooms

2 tablespoons butter

2 tablespoons canola oil

1 bunch scallions, trimmed, rinsed, and thinly sliced (include 1 inch of the green)

1 pound presliced white button mushrooms, rinsed and dried with paper towels

1 tablespoon quinoa flour

½ cup low-salt vegetable bouillon, or more as needed

1 cup sour cream

2 tablespoons snipped fresh dill

½ teaspoon salt

¼ teaspoon freshly ground black pepper

2 tablespoons dry sherry

Pinch sweet paprika (optional)

1. **For Polenta:** In a 3-quart saucepan over medium heat, bring water, salt, bay leaf, and garlic to a boil. Gradually pour polenta, in a showerlike fashion, into the boiling water, whisking constantly until polenta thickens, about 5 minutes. (Though thicker, it will still be runny.) Discard bay leaf and garlic. Add Basic Boiled Quinoa, and stir until well blended. Cook until mixture reaches desired consistency (soft or hard), 10–15 minutes (but judge by texture, not time). Mix in the cheese. Add salt and pepper to taste. Transfer to a buttered shallow pan and keep warm.

2. **For Creamed Mushrooms:** Heat butter and oil in a large sauté or frying pan over medium heat. Add scallions and cook, stirring, for 2 minutes. Add mushrooms and cook until tender and half of the liquid that mushrooms exude has evaporated, about 5 minutes. Sprinkle quinoa flour over mushrooms and cook, stirring, for 1 minute. Add vegetable bouillon, sour cream, dill, salt, pepper, and sherry, and cook for 1 minute. Note: The amount of broth to add depends on whether you prefer a thin or thick sauce. Start with ½ cup and add more if you want a thinner sauce.

3. To complete, cut the polenta into 4 pieces and place each piece on a plate. Top with ¼ of the mushroom sauce, and sprinkle with paprika. I like to serve this with asparagus or green beans dressed with lemon juice and chives.

Potato and Kañiwa Torte

Potato tortes are everyday fare in the Andean countries, where the potato is king, and when paired with kañiwa, they make a great meatless meal. I especially like to serve this dish with tomatoes diced about ¼ inch and quickly sautéed in a teaspoon of oil. For meat lovers, you can add Canadian ham or prosciutto, finely chopped. And, since this dish is rich in vitamin C and calcium and has good amounts of potassium, iron, zinc, vitamin A, and the B vitamins, it's nutritious and delicious!

YIELDS 6 SERVINGS

1 pound all-purpose potatoes, well cleaned

2 cups Basic Boiled Kañiwa (see recipe in Chapter 1; 2 cups of Basic Boiled Quinoa can also be used)

4 tablespoons butter

½ cup low-fat warm milk mixed with ½ teaspoon paprika

¼ cup finely chopped Canadian bacon or prosciutto (optional)

⅓ cup minced scallions

2 cloves garlic, passed through a garlic press

¼ cup minced fresh parsley leaves

¼ teaspoon freshly ground black pepper

¼ cup rice flour or cornstarch mixed with 1 teaspoon baking powder

1 cup firmly packed, shredded soft fontina or any other good melting cheese

3 large eggs, lightly beaten, mixed with ¼ cup milk

¼ cup grated Parmesan cheese

1. Cook potatoes in boiling salted water as for mashed potatoes, about 15–20 minutes, or until soft. Let potatoes cool until you can handle them, cut in half, and pass through a ricer, if available. Otherwise peel and mash with butter and milk mixed with paprika. Mix with rest of ingredients except Parmesan cheese.

2. Preheat the oven to 375°F and butter a 7" × 11" baking pan (or a 9" × 9" pan). Transfer potato mixture into baking pan, sprinkle with Parmesan cheese, and bake for 45 minutes or until golden brown. Cool for 10 minutes and cut into 12 pieces. Serve 2 pieces with a side dish of green bean and tomato salad or sautéed diced tomatoes.

Mexican Casserole

This delicious casserole combines the layering of a lasagna, the flavors of Mexico, and the nutritional boost offered by quinoa. Instead of noodles, use fried, rectangular corn chip strips from the snack aisle to create the layers. This dish is close to irresistible.

YIELDS 6–8 SERVINGS

1½ cups chunky corn and black bean salsa, divided

3 cups rectangular, fried corn chips (chips should be about 3" × 1")

1 cup cooked chicken, cut into 1-inch cubes

1 cup Basic Boiled Quinoa (see recipe in Chapter 1)

1 cup sour cream (regular or low-fat)

1 cup shredded Chihuahua cheese, plain or with jalapeño, divided

1 cup shredded Cheddar cheese, divided

1 (4-ounce) can chopped green chilies

1 teaspoon ground chili powder

¼ teaspoon cayenne pepper

½ cup heavy cream (optional)

1. Preheat the oven to 350°F.

2. Coat a 9" × 9" or 7" × 11" baking dish with cooking spray. Spread ½ cup of the chunky salsa on the bottom of the baking dish. Then cover the salsa with a layer of corn chips.

3. In a large bowl, combine chicken, Basic Boiled Quinoa, sour cream, ¾ cup Chihuahua cheese, ¾ cup Cheddar cheese, ½ cup salsa, chilies, chili powder, and cayenne pepper. Mix well to combine.

4. Spread chicken mixture over the layer of corn chips and smooth with the back of a spoon, to create an even layer. Cover the chicken with another layer of corn chips. Drizzle the remaining salsa over the chips, and top with the remaining ¼ cup Chihuahua cheese and ¼ cup Cheddar. If a richer casserole is desired, spoon the cream around the edges of the casserole.

5. Cover with foil and bake for 30 minutes. Remove the foil and bake 15 minutes more, until top is golden and bubbly. Let stand for 5 minutes before serving.

➤ KITCHEN WISDOM

Because corn chips come in bags that hold more than 3 cups, you should have no problem getting the right number. Select 32–36 unbroken chips for the recipe (number may vary depending on size of pan you use), and then enjoy the rest with one of the dips in Chapter 4.

Stewed Fish Caribbean Style

This particular version of stewed fish is typical of many Caribbean countries and can be made with any white, firm fish, such as cod, turbot, halibut, catfish, or any other lean fish. Meaty fish such as mahi-mahi is also excellent, but, depending on the thickness, will probably need a longer cooking time. The sauce can be made ahead and the dish finished just a few minutes before serving.

YIELDS 4 SERVINGS

4 boneless fillets (about 4 ounces each) white, firm fish

Juice of 1 lemon (about 2 tablespoons)

Salt and freshly ground black pepper

1 tablespoon extra-virgin olive oil

1 teaspoon sweet paprika

1 small onion, halved and thinly sliced

3 cloves garlic, passed through a garlic press

1 pound firm tomatoes, peeled, seeded, and cut into strips

½ cup pimento strips

1 tablespoon tomato paste

Pinch sugar

6 large fresh basil leaves, julienned, or ½ teaspoon dried basil

2 cups Basic Boiled Quinoa (see recipe in Chapter 1)

1 pound baby yellow or red potatoes, cooked

2 tablespoons fresh minced parsley leaves

1. Cut each fish fillet in half. Sprinkle fillets with lemon juice and salt and pepper to taste. Let stand at room temperature while preparing the sauce.

2. In a large skillet, heat oil over medium-low heat. Add paprika, onions, and garlic. Cook, stirring, for 2 minutes. Add tomatoes, pimentos, tomato paste, sugar, and basil, and cook, stirring, for 3 minutes. Add salt and pepper to taste. Sauce can be made ahead to this point, then cooled and refrigerated in a covered container until needed.

3. To finish preparing the dish, bring sauce to room temperature and heat to a boil over medium heat. Arrange fish fillets on top of sauce, reduce heat to low, cover, and simmer until fish is firm to the touch, about 8–10 minutes, or bake, covered, in a preheated 350°F oven for about 10 minutes, depending on the thickness of the fillets. Remove fillets to a heated platter and keep in warming oven. If sauce is too watery, reduce over high heat, adding any juices the fish may release. Add salt, pepper, and sugar to taste.

4. To serve, put ½ cup Basic Boiled Quinoa in the bottom of a soup plate, top with 2 pieces of fish, cover with sauce, arrange potatoes (tossed in 1 tablespoon butter, if desired) around, and sprinkle with parsley. A vegetable such as broccoli or zucchini would complement the meal very nicely.

➤ BACKGROUND INFORMATION

You probably know that you should eat more fish to get those important omega-3 fatty acids. Dishes like this make that a lot easier. This stew is also rich in potassium and niacin as well as vitamins A, C, B_1, B_6, and B_{12}; it also has good amounts of iron, zinc, vitamin B_2, and folate.

STEWED FISH CARIBBEAN STYLE

Corn Torte

This Paraguayan Corn Torte is a wonderful dish with big flavor and a luxurious mouthfeel. Red quinoa blends beautifully in this dish, which can be used as a main course for lunch paired with a leafy greens salads and a cup of soup, or as a side dish at dinner, with grilled poultry, meat, or fish. Whichever way you use it, it is always a hit. In addition to flavor, it also provides good amounts of iron and vitamins A and B_2.

YIELDS 6 SERVINGS

1 cup thinly sliced onions

1 cup thinly sliced leeks (use white part with 1 inch of green)

1 teaspoon salt

½ cup quinoa flour

2 teaspoons baking powder

1 teaspoon sugar

1 (20-ounce) package frozen sweet corn, thawed

8 tablespoons unsalted butter, melted

3 egg yolks

½ cup milk

8 ounces (about 2 cups) shredded fontina cheese

1 cup Basic Boiled Quinoa (see recipe in Chapter 1; red quinoa is recommended)

3 egg whites

2 tablespoons freshly grated Parmesan cheese

1. Preheat the oven to 375°F. In a small saucepan, bring 1 cup water to a boil. Add onions, leeks, and salt; cover, and simmer for 10 minutes. Cool.

2. Combine quinoa flour, baking powder, and sugar. In a food processor, purée corn until smooth. Add butter, egg yolks, quinoa flour mixture, and milk, and process until well mixed. Add cheese, and pulse processor until ingredients are well blended. Transfer to a large mixing bowl, add Basic Boiled Quinoa and onion mixture, and mix well.

3. In a separate bowl, beat egg whites until stiff but not dry. Carefully fold into the corn mixture. Turn into a 9" × 9" or a 7" × 11" buttered baking dish, sprinkle with Parmesan cheese, and bake in the middle of the oven for 45 minutes or until golden brown. Remove from the oven and let rest for 5 minutes before cutting into serving portions.

CABBAGE PATTIES WITH QUINOA, CHICKEN, AND AMARANTH

Cabbage Patties with Quinoa, Chicken, and Amaranth

If you're a lover of Eastern European cooking, you will appreciate this easy recipe that gives all the taste and none of the hassle of traditional stuffed cabbage rolls. Forget arranging filling on fragile leaves and tying everything up with strings, and give this simple patty mixture a try! In this recipe, quinoa replaces the traditional white rice to help bind the patties, as well as to provide extra nutrition. In addition to abundant protein and fiber, this dish is rich in iron and vitamins C and B_6, folate, and niacin, and offers good amounts of potassium, zinc, and vitamins B_1 and B_2.

YIELDS 8 PATTIES, 2 PATTIES PER SERVING

4 cups finely chopped savoy cabbage

½ pound lean ground chicken or turkey

2 large eggs lightly beaten

2 cloves garlic, passed through a garlic press

1 small onion, minced (about ½ cup)

½ teaspoon salt

¼ teaspoon freshly ground black pepper

Pinch nutmeg

2 tablespoons minced fresh parsley

2 tablespoons or more amaranth flakes

2 cups Basic Boiled Quinoa (see recipe in Chapter 1)

Olive oil spray

1. Steam or cook cabbage in boiling water for 10 minutes or until tender. Drain thoroughly and let cool.

2. Mix ground chicken or turkey with eggs, garlic, onion, salt, pepper, nutmeg, parsley, and amaranth flakes, kneading until well blended. Add Basic Boiled Quinoa and cabbage, mix well, and shape into 8 patties. Spray oil over a large, heavy skillet and heat over medium heat. Add patties and cook until browned on both sides, about 4 minutes on each side. If frying pan is not large enough to hold 8 patties without crowding, cook in two batches. Drain on paper towels and keep warm in a warming oven until ready to serve.

➤ VARIATIONS

If the patties are very moist, you can dip them in amaranth flour before frying.

Quinoa Macaroni and Broccoli Gratinée

This is a great dish suited for any occasion, plus it is easily transformed with available ingredients. For example, it can be made with any kind of pasta, and small cauliflower florets can be used instead of broccoli. It can also be made ahead. If you're looking to add some extra flavor, try adding a little cream, which also helps create a more delicate sauce. This dish is also rich in calcium and vitamin B_2, with good amounts of iron, zinc, and vitamins A and B_1.

YIELDS 6 SERVINGS

2 cups 1% low-fat milk, or favorite milk

3 tablespoons butter, divided

2 tablespoons quinoa flour

½ teaspoon salt

¼ teaspoon ground white pepper

Pinch nutmeg

Pinch sugar

¼ cup whipping cream, plus additional ¼ cup, if desired

1 (10-ounce) package frozen broccoli, thawed, drained, and coarsely chopped

1 cup frozen peas, thawed and drained

2 tablespoons minced fresh parsley leaves

1 (8-ounce) package quinoa macaroni

4 ounces grated mozzarella cheese

½ cup grated Parmesan cheese

1. Heat the milk in a small saucepan. In a heavy 2-quart saucepan, melt 2 tablespoons butter over medium heat. Add flour and cook, stirring, for 1 minute. Do not let it brown. Remove from the heat and whisk in the hot milk; return to the heat and bring to a boil, stirring constantly. Season with salt, pepper, nutmeg, and sugar, and simmer for 5 minutes over low heat. Add cream and mix well. Set aside, covered with a round of wax paper.

2. In a medium skillet, melt 1 tablespoon butter over medium heat. Add broccoli and peas and cook, stirring, for 1 minute. Toss with parsley and the cream sauce.

3. In a 4-quart saucepan, cook pasta according to package directions, stirring to separate the macaroni. Cook al dente. (*Al dente* is Italian for "to the tooth," which means that pasta should be cooked until tender but still firm. There should be a little resistance when you bite down on it.) Drain and rinse. Set aside.

4. Butter a 6-cup shallow ovenproof dish (round or rectangular). Mix together the cheeses. Layer one half each of pasta, vegetables, and cheese mixture. Repeat with the other half of each, finishing with a layer of cheese. Drizzle additional ¼ cup cream around the inside of dish to prevent the sauce from drying, if desired. Can be prepared ahead to this point, covered, and refrigerated.

5. To serve, bring dish to room temperature and preheat the oven to 375°F. Bake dish in the upper third of the oven for 20 minutes. Put under broiler for 5 seconds, until lightly browned. Be careful not to let sauce dry. Let sit for 5 minutes, cut into 6 pieces, and serve immediately.

QUINOA MACARONI AND BROCCOLI GRATINÉE

Quinoa Fettuccine with Ham Sauce

This is a very simple pasta dish, which is very popular in most of South America. It is flavorful and wholesome, and loved by children and adults alike. Rich in vitamins B_1 and B_2, niacin, and iron, it also has good quantities of calcium, potassium, zinc, and vitamins A, B_6, and B_{12}.

YIELDS 4 SERVINGS

1 (8-ounce) package quinoa fettuccine

2 tablespoons unsalted butter

1 (⅛-inch thick) slice boiled ham, chopped

2 ounces canned minced mushrooms

½ cup milk

½ cup grated fontina or Gouda cheese

2 hard-boiled eggs, peeled and chopped

2 tablespoons minced fresh parsley leaves

Parmesan cheese, optional

1. Cook pasta al dente according to package directions. (*Al dente* is Italian for "to the tooth," which means that pasta should be cooked until tender but still firm. There should be a little resistance when you bite down on it.) Drain pasta, reserving some of the water. Keep warm.

2. In a heavy 10-inch skillet, melt butter over low heat. Add ham and mushrooms and cook for 2 minutes. Add milk, cheese, and chopped eggs; heat mixture through without letting it boil. If too thick, add a little of the pasta cooking water.

3. When ready to serve, transfer pasta to a serving bowl, pour sauce over it, and sprinkle with parsley and Parmesan cheese, if desired. Serve immediately.

CHAPTER 7
Desserts

Desserts occupy a special place in the hearts of most people around the globe, and the ancient grains make it possible to create sweets that have more fiber, protein, and nutrients than you might expect. This doesn't make these desserts "health foods," but it does mean you might be able to enjoy them without feeling too guilty.

My greatest challenge has been to come up with great, easy dessert recipes that are more healthful than many of today's sweets. Of course, there is fruit, and that is always a good choice, but sometimes you want something a little special. While it is impossible to completely eliminate sugar, I have worked to reduce it when possible and have used more wholesome options, such as raw sugar, whenever possible. However, butter is almost impossible to cut down if you want to make delicious cookies and pastries. My advice is to make things wonderful and then use moderation when consuming cookies and sweets.

QUINOA BARS WITH KAÑIWA

Quinoa Bars with Kañiwa

This particular recipe was inspired by a sweet quinoa tamale found in my native Ecuador. Here, cinnamon combines with cloves and anise to give these moist, cakelike bars a decided holiday tone. But even though they're perfect for the holidays, they are versatile enough to suit any occasion. Stamina seekers, from hikers to woodchoppers, will especially appreciate the mix of nuts and dried fruit. A certain winner with anyone, these nutritious bars will quickly disappear from your serving platter.

YIELDS 24 SERVINGS

1 cup quinoa, thoroughly rinsed

2 cups water

1 cup raw sugar

1 cup rice flour or cornstarch

1 teaspoon baking powder

½ teaspoon baking soda

1 teaspoon ground cinnamon

½ teaspoon ground cloves

¼ teaspoon nutmeg

1 teaspoon anise seeds, crushed

½ cup seedless black or gold raisins

½ cup coarsely chopped dates or dry apricots

1½ cups chopped walnuts

½ cup Basic Boiled Kañiwa (see recipe in Chapter 1)

4 ounces (1 stick) unsalted butter, melted and cooled

½ cup orange juice

2 teaspoons vanilla extract

3 large eggs, lightly beaten

Confectioners' sugar for dusting (optional)

1. Preheat the oven to 350°F.

2. Put quinoa and water in saucepan, bring to a boil, and cook for 12 minutes or until all the water has been absorbed. Remove from the heat, fluff with a fork, cover, and let cool.

3. In a large mixing bowl, combine sugar, rice flour, baking powder, baking soda, cinnamon, cloves, nutmeg, anise seeds, raisins, apricots, walnuts, and Basic Boiled Kañiwa; mix well. Add cooked quinoa, butter, orange juice, vanilla, and eggs, and mix thoroughly. Transfer to a buttered and floured 13" × 9" baking pan.

4. Bake in the upper third of the oven for 45 minutes, or until a toothpick inserted in the center comes out clean. Cool on a wire rack.

5. Cut into 24 bars. If desired, dust with confectioners' sugar before serving.

CHOCOLATE TRIANGLES WITH QUINOA FLOUR

Chocolate Triangles with Quinoa Flour

These wonderful cookies have been part of our Christmas cookie tray for more years than I care to remember. They are easy and fast to make and store well. I tried to reduce the amount of sugar, but it made these triangles soft, not crispy as they should be. Organic cane sugar is a healthier choice than white sugar, and in this case it doesn't interfere with the taste of the cookie.

YIELDS 24 COOKIES, 2 COOKIES PER SERVING

1 ounce unsweetened chocolate, cut up in small pieces

4 tablespoons (½ stick) unsalted butter

½ cup organic cane sugar

1 large egg, unbeaten

¼ cup quinoa flour

Pinch salt

¼ teaspoon vanilla extract

⅓ cup finely chopped walnuts, pistachio nuts, or pecans

1. Preheat the oven to 400°F.

2. In a small saucepan, melt chocolate and butter over low heat, stirring so it melts evenly. As soon as this mixture begins to melt, add sugar. Remove from the heat, and continue to stir until it is all melted.

3. Add egg, quinoa flour, salt, and vanilla extract. With a wooden spoon, beat until mixture is smooth.

4. Lightly grease a 13" × 9" × 1" jellyroll pan and spread chocolate mixture evenly. Then sprinkle with nuts. Bake for 12 minutes or until the mixture starts pulling away from the sides.

5. Cool slightly, cut into 2-inch squares, then cut into triangles. Be sure to cut while still quite hot. Once cold, remove from the pan and store in an airtight container.

Quinoa Brown Sugar Nut Balls

Quinoa's talent for producing a flour with character is brought to the fore in these crunchy palate pleasers. The ground almonds add a bit more fiber and nutrition, as well as great taste. I like to serve these for afternoon tea or as a snack before bedtime, with a glass of milk.

YIELDS 60, 2 PER SERVING

2 sticks (8 ounces) unsalted butter, softened

½ cup (packed) organic light brown sugar

2 teaspoons vanilla extract

2 cups quinoa flour

½ cup finely ground almonds

½ cup confectioners' sugar for dusting

1. Preheat the oven to 325°F.

2. In the large bowl of an electric mixer, beat the butter until fluffy. Add brown sugar and vanilla extract, and beat until well blended. Combine flour and ground almonds, and gradually add the flour and nut mixture to the butter (add in about 3 parts).

3. Chill the dough if too soft to handle. When dough is firm, shape into 1-inch balls or crescents. Place on ungreased cookie sheets and bake for 12 minutes or until lightly browned. Cool on racks and dust with confectioners' sugar while warm.

Mango Parfait with Chia Seeds

I grew up eating mangoes, and when they are in season, I eat them frequently, either plain or in salads and desserts. Recently, I was reading a recipe for mango lassi, an Indian drink made from mango, yogurt, water, and ice. This brought to mind the idea that Brazilians mix the purée of either mango or papaya with ice cream and drizzle it with crème de cassis. I combined these ideas in this light, refreshing Mango Parfait with Chia Seeds. As you make this recipe, keep in mind that if the mangoes are very sweet, you won't need to add much sugar. If the mangoes aren't sweet, start with 1 tablespoon sugar, and then add confectioners' sugar to taste. The crystallized orange peel and the coconut also provide sweetness to this delicious dish.

YIELDS 4 SERVINGS

2 large, ripe mangoes

1 cup plain Greek yogurt

1 tablespoon lemon juice

1 tablespoon raw sugar or organic cane sugar

¼ teaspoon vanilla extract

2 tablespoons raw chia seeds

4 tablespoons finely chopped crystallized orange peel

1 tablespoon crème de cassis (optional)

Confectioners' sugar to taste

1 cup blueberries, fresh or frozen

1 cup fresh sliced strawberries

½ cup angel flake coconut

1. Peel mangoes, remove the pulp with a small sharp knife, chop coarsely, and purée in a food processor. Add yogurt, lemon juice, sugar, and vanilla, and purée until smooth and creamy. Transfer to a nonmetallic bowl and mix with the raw chia seeds, orange peel, and optional crème de cassis. Taste for sweetness, and if needed, add confectioners' sugar to taste. Cover and refrigerate for 2–3 hours.

2. Combine the blueberries and strawberries. To serve, divide the berries among 4 stemmed glasses, and top the berries with ½ cup of the mango cream. Garnish with 2 tablespoons coconut.

➤ VARIATIONS

I use raw chia seeds when I want a thicker mango purée, since chia seeds absorb a lot of moisture. Remember, however, that cooked grains, rather than raw chia, are generally recommended for people who have digestive problems. If you need to swap out the chia, substitute ¼ cup Basic Boiled Kañiwa (see recipe in Chapter 1) instead. This makes the parfait a little lighter.

AMARANTH AND CORNSTARCH DAINTIES

Amaranth and Cornstarch Dainties

Who says healthy food can't make a great-tasting snack? In this recipe, amaranth flour lightened with cornstarch and rice flour makes a wonderful, light cookie that would be at home on the shelves of the finest pastry shops. Not too sweet, these delights are airy and aromatic with vanilla, and they are perfect for afternoon coffee.

YIELDS 2 DOZEN COOKIES, 2 PER SERVING

1 stick (4 ounces) unsalted butter, softened

¼ cup confectioners' sugar

1 teaspoon vanilla extract

½ cup cornstarch

¼ cup rice flour

¼ cup amaranth flour

¼ cup cinnamon sugar for dusting

1. Preheat the oven to 275°F. In the large bowl of a mixer, beat butter until fluffy. Add sugar and vanilla extract, and beat until well blended. Combine cornstarch, rice flour, and amaranth flour, and gradually add to butter (add in about 3 parts). Chill the dough for 1 hour or until stiff enough to handle.

2. Shape dough into 1-inch balls. Place on ungreased cookie sheets about 2 inches apart. Dip the tines of a fork in flour and press the balls to flatten.

3. Bake for 30 minutes or until cooked throughout. Cookies should not color. Cool on racks and dust with cinnamon sugar while warm.

COCONUT, TAPIOCA, AND KAÑIWA CAKE WITH CHOCOLATE HAZELNUT SAUCE

Coconut, Tapioca, and Kañiwa Cake
with Chocolate Hazelnut Sauce

Brazilians love sweets, especially those made with coconut. Tapioca, made from the cassava root, is also much loved in Brazil, where this dessert is served for teatime with either tea or a cup of coffee. This dish combines these two ingredients in an amazingly delicious cake. It can be made in a cake pan or in a pie dish, or in a springform pan, which is what I prefer. This is a real treat for coconut lovers.

YIELDS 12 SERVINGS

Chocolate Hazelnut Sauce

1 (8-ounce) jar chocolate hazelnut spread

½ cup heavy cream

2 tablespoons brandy

Cake

1 cup packed fresh grated coconut, or frozen, thawed (about 5 ounces)

1 cup minute tapioca

¾ cup Basic Boiled Kañiwa (see recipe in Chapter 1; if Basic Boiled Kañiwa is not available, substitute an equal amount of Basic Boiled Quinoa from Chapter 1)

1 cup low-fat milk (or any milk of your preference)

½ cup sugar

½ teaspoon salt

1 cup unsweetened coconut milk

1 recipe Chocolate Hazelnut Sauce

1 pint assorted berries

1. **For Chocolate Hazelnut Sauce:** Bring 1 inch of water to a simmer in the bottom pan of a double boiler. Place chocolate hazelnut spread and cream in the top pan of the double boiler and heat, stirring occasionally, until sauce is well mixed and melted. Stir in brandy. Let cool and transfer to a serving bowl.

2. **For Cake:** In a medium bowl, mix coconut, tapioca, and Basic Boiled Kañiwa. In a small saucepan, combine milk, sugar, and salt, and bring to a boil, stirring until the sugar is dissolved. Stir in coconut milk, and pour over tapioca mixture. Stir with a wooden spoon until well mixed. Moisten an 8-inch round mold with cold water and pour in the mixture. Cover and let stand for at least 4 hours at room temperature or refrigerate overnight.

3. To serve, turn onto a serving platter and cut into 12 pieces. Serve each piece on a dessert plate, drizzle the chocolate sauce on top, and scatter the berries around the cake.

➤ VARIATIONS

If using desiccated coconut, soak in a little milk or water to restore some of the freshness. You can also use sweetened angel flake coconut, but reduce the amount of sugar (about ¼ cup to ⅓ cup, depending on how sweet you like your desserts). Remember, the chocolate sauce provides additional sweetness, so feel free to skip the sauce and garnish with extra coconut instead if you don't want your dessert to be super sweet.

Dates Stuffed with Nuts and Chia Seeds

Around the Christmas holidays, it is possible to find Medjool dates that are so soft they ooze sugary syrup. This is the time when I make stuffed dates. The filling is traditionally made with almonds and sometimes with pistachios. Because pistachios are pricier in the Middle East, many people there tint the almonds to make them look like pistachios. The freshness and moisture level of the nuts varies, so add Chia Gel 1 tablespoon at a time until the mixture is soft enough to shape into a log.

YIELDS 24 SERVINGS

4 ounces peeled almonds (about 1 cup)

2–4 tablespoons Chia Gel (see recipe in Chapter 1)

1 tablespoon honey or agave nectar

1 teaspoon vanilla extract or rosewater

24 large Medjool dates

1. Place nuts in a food processor and blend until they form a paste, adding a little water if too dry. Transfer mixture to a bowl and mix with Chia Gel, honey, and vanilla extract or rosewater; knead into a smooth paste. Shape paste into 2 logs, about 1 inch in diameter, and cut each log into 12 pieces.

2. Remove pits from dates, and fill the empty space in each date with a piece of paste, closing ends so nut paste is visible.

3. To serve, place filled dates in decorative paper cups. Serve immediately. If not serving right away, store (without the paper cups) in tins layered with waxed paper. Cover tightly and store at room temperature for 1 or 2 days, in the refrigerator for up to 2 weeks, or in the freezer for up to 2 months.

Berries with Coconut Yogurt and Kañiwa

This type of fruit salad is one of the best; it is beautiful to look at and delicious and refreshing any time of day, thanks in part to the delicious yogurt used in this recipe. The coconut yogurt (made with coconut milk) is new in the market and not all stores carry it so far, but it is worth searching out for a change of pace. The texture is thinner than regular yogurt, and it has a coconut taste and natural sweetness that can make up for the lack of sweetness in some fruits. The Vanilla Coconut Yogurt Cream that tops this recipe can be used on other desserts, such as the Baby Bananas with Orange Sauce found in this chapter. I usually serve this fruit salad after a heavy meal, accompanied by either the Amaranth and Cornstarch Dainties or Quinoa Brown Sugar Nut Balls found in this chapter.

YIELDS 8 SERVINGS

Vanilla Coconut Yogurt Cream

1 cup vanilla-flavored coconut yogurt

½ cup plain Greek yogurt

¼ cup heavy cream

¼ cup Basic Boiled Kañiwa (see recipe in Chapter 1)

Orange Berries

4 cups mixed fresh berries, well rinsed and dried

2 tablespoons orange juice

Freshly grated lemon peel (optional)

Lightly Toasted Chia Seeds (see recipe in Chapter 1) (optional)

1. **For Vanilla Coconut Yogurt Cream:** In a medium bowl, mix the two yogurts, heavy cream, and Basic Boiled Kañiwa.

2. **For Orange Berries:** In a large glass bowl, mix the berries with the orange juice. Chill until needed.

3. To serve, place ½ cup of the berry mixture in a small glass bowl or stemmed dessert glass. Top with ¼ cup of the yogurt mixture. Garnish with lemon peel and Toasted Chia Seeds, if desired.

➤ VARIATIONS

For a fancier dinner party, when serving this dessert to adults I often substitute Grand Marnier for the orange juice.

BABY BANANAS WITH ORANGE SAUCE

Baby Bananas with Orange Sauce

Latin Americans excel at confections made with different kinds of bananas. This is one of my favorites, because it takes only a few minutes to prepare and it is absolutely delicious. Baby bananas (also called niños or ladyfingers) aren't really babies. They are a different, much smaller, and sweeter variety of banana than the ones commonly eaten in the United States. They are often carried by mainstream grocers, but will certainly be found in Hispanic stores.

YIELDS 4 SERVINGS

2 tablespoons unsalted butter

8 ripe but firm baby bananas, peeled

4 tablespoons light brown sugar, preferably raw

4 tablespoons orange juice or dark rum

Toasted Chia Seeds (see recipe in Chapter 1), for garnish

Toasted unsweetened coconut, for garnish

Vanilla Coconut Yogurt Cream (see Berries with Coconut Yogurt and Kañiwa recipe in this chapter) or ice cream, for garnish (optional)

1. In a heavy skillet large enough to hold the 8 bananas, heat the butter over low heat. Add bananas and cook on all sides until lightly browned. Sprinkle sugar and orange juice or rum on top and cook, shaking the skillet often, until the sugar is melted.

2. Remove pan from the heat. Carefully roll each banana in the sauce in the pan. Serve 2 bananas on each dessert plate, topped with Toasted Chia Seeds and/or toasted coconut. A dollop of Vanilla Coconut Yogurt Cream or a scoop of ice cream are also great ways to finish this dessert.

APPENDIX A
Resource List

WHERE TO FIND THE GRAINS

Quinoa and amaranth have long been available in health food and natural food stores. Chia seeds have begun appearing in recent years, as well. With the increased interest in these super grains, these three are now also available in many mainstream supermarket chains and even appear on the shelves of warehouse clubs. The greatest range of colors or forms is likely to be in natural foods stores, but a good variety can also usually be found in specialty stores, such as Trader Joe's. The grains are usually packaged, but natural foods stores, such as Whole Foods, often have at least quinoa in their bulk foods section. These are becoming sufficiently popular that you may never need to search farther than your regular grocery store.

Kañiwa, which is a more recent introduction in the United States, may not be as readily available in stores, but it, along with the other grains, can easily be found on the Internet. With this grain, you may have to get creative in your searches, as there are so many different spellings. Try *kanihua, canigua, cañihua,* or *kaniwa,* if *kañiwa* doesn't turn up what you want.

Here are some sites where you may find these grains:

Alter Eco (*www.alterecofoods.com*) offers black quinoa, red quinoa, and rainbow quinoa.

Amazon (*www.amazon.com*) has all four grains available in its grocery section. In addition to having the grains, it has multiple forms of the grains: whole, flakes, flour, and, in the case of quinoa, pasta as well.

Ancient Harvest Quinoa (*http://store.ancientharvestquinoa.com*) sells quinoa grain, flour, flakes, and pasta, as well as the corn-quinoa pasta suggested in some of the recipes in this book.

Bob's Red Mill (*www.bobsredmill.com*) and Arrowhead Mills (*www.arrowheadmills.com*) are major natural/organic grain mills. They both have quinoa and amaranth, and Bob's Red Mill has chia seeds, as well.

Igourmet.com (*www.igourmet.com*) features many of the brands mentioned here, and all four of the grains, including organic chia seeds.

Nuchia Foods Corporation (*www.nuchiafoodscorporation.com*) offers chia seeds and chia seed flour, as well as more information on the wonders of chia seeds.

The Nuts.com (*www.nuts.com*) site does not yet have kañiwa, but it does have the other three grains in a wide range of forms, as well as a tremendous number of other gluten-free grains and seeds.

Roland Food (*www.rolandfood.com*) has all four grains, and also has the tricolor quinoa suggested in a few recipes in this book.

Walmart (*www.walmart.com*) has amaranth and quinoa listed under Grocery and chia seeds under Health. However, kañiwa has not yet appeared on the Walmart site.

Zocalo Gourmet (*www.zocalogourmet.com*) has kañiwa grain and flour, as well as amaranth and quinoa.

These sites and sources give you a lot of options to get you started with exploration and comparison shopping. However, this list is not exhaustive. You may find a wonderful source right in your neighborhood.

WHERE TO FIND INFORMATION

There are many sources for additional information on these grains. I have mentioned several excellent books in discussing these grains, but you can find more on these and other super foods on the Internet. For example, Peruvian Superfood (*www.peruviansuperfood.com*) is a site that discusses kañiwa and quinoa from a Peruvian perspective, including how these grains (and other Peruvian superfoods) are used by chefs in Peru. The international readership of this site also underscores how widespread interest in these grains has become. Learn more about the ancient grains here:

Chia: Rediscovering a Forgotten Crop of the Aztecs by Dr. Wayne Coates and Ricardo Ayerza
Quinoa, the Supergrain: Ancient Food for Today by Rebecca Wood
The Art of Cooking with Quinoa by Maria Baez Kijac
The Magic of Chia by James F. Scheer
The South American Table by Maria Baez Kijac
Whole Grains Every Day, Every Way by Lorna Sass

Metric Conversion Chart

VOLUME CONVERSIONS

U.S. Volume Measure	Metric Equivalent
⅛ teaspoon	0.5 milliliters
¼ teaspoon	1 milliliters
½ teaspoon	2 milliliters
1 teaspoon	5 milliliters
½ tablespoon	7 milliliters
1 tablespoon (3 teaspoons)	15 milliliters
2 tablespoons (1 fluid ounce)	30 milliliters
¼ cup (4 tablespoons)	60 milliliters
⅓ cup	90 milliliters
½ cup (4 fluid ounces)	125 milliliters
⅔ cup	160 milliliters
¾ cup (6 fluid ounces)	180 milliliters
1 cup (16 tablespoons)	250 milliliters
1 pint (2 cups)	500 milliliters
1 quart (4 cups)	1 liter (about)

WEIGHT CONVERSIONS

U.S. Weight Measure	Metric Equivalent
½ ounce	15 grams
1 ounce	30 grams
2 ounces	60 grams
3 ounces	85 grams
¼ pound (4 ounces)	115 grams
½ pound (8 ounces)	225 grams
¾ pound (12 ounces)	340 grams
1 pound (16 ounces)	454 grams

OVEN TEMPERATURE CONVERSIONS

Degrees Fahrenheit	Degrees Celsius
200 degrees F	95 degrees C
250 degrees F	120 degrees C
275 degrees F	135 degrees C
300 degrees F	150 degrees C
325 degrees F	160 degrees C
350 degrees F	180 degrees C
375 degrees F	190 degrees C
400 degrees F	205 degrees C
425 degrees F	220 degrees C
450 degrees F	230 degrees C

BAKING PAN SIZES

American	Metric
8 × 1½ inch round baking pan	20 × 4 cm cake tin
9 × 1½ inch round baking pan	23 × 3.5 cm cake tin
11 × 7 × 1½ inch baking pan	28 × 18 × 4 cm baking tin
13 × 9 × 2 inch baking pan	30 × 20 × 5 cm baking tin
2 quart rectangular baking dish	30 × 20 × 3 cm baking tin
15 × 10 × 2 inch baking pan	30 × 25 × 2 cm baking tin (Swiss roll tin)
9 inch pie plate	22 × 4 or 23 × 4 cm pie plate
7 or 8 inch springform pan	18 or 20 cm springform or loose bottom cake tin
9 × 5 × 3 inch loaf pan	23 × 13 × 7 cm or 2 lb narrow loaf or pâté tin
1½ quart casserole	1.5 liter casserole
2 quart casserole	2 liter casserole

Index

Note: Page numbers in *italics* indicate photographs.

About the Author

A native of Quito, Ecuador, Maria Baez Kijac is a food writer, historian, and former culinary teacher who specializes in Latin American cuisine. She is the author of *Cooking with a Latin Beat*, *The Art of Cooking with Quinoa*, and *The South American Table*—which was named the best Latin American Cookbook of 2003 by the Gourmand World Cookbook Awards and, in 2012, was named by *Cooking Light* magazine one of the top 100 cookbooks of the last 25 years. Maria has done research and studied cooking in Spain, Portugal, and many Latin American countries. Maria was also the kitchen director for the *American Family Kitchen*, a TV series produced by PBS. She is a longtime member of the International Association of Culinary Professionals (IACP) and the Culinary Historians of Chicago, and was a member of the jury for the Slow Food Award for the Defense of Biodiversity. She was also a member of the Food Futurists (who predict future trends in food) for the Food Channel's *TrendWire* newsletter and has written articles for *Cooking Light* and *FamilyFun* magazines. Maria lives in Vernon Hills, Illinois.